Reflections From Captivity

Southeast Asia Translation Series
Volume I

Phan Boi Chau's 'Prison Notes'
Ho Chi Minh's 'Prison Diary'

REFLECTIONS FROM CAPTIVITY

Translated by
Christopher Jenkins, Tran Khanh Tuyet,
and Huynh Sanh Thong
Edited by David G. Marr

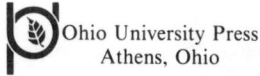
Ohio University Press
Athens, Ohio

Library of Congress Cataloging in Publication Data

Main entry under title:

Reflections from captivity.

(Translations Project Group series ; v. 1)
Translation of Phan Boi Chau's *Nguc trung thu* and of Ho Chi Minh's *Nhat ky trong tu.*
Includes bibliographical references and index.
CONTENTS: Phan Boi Chau. Prison Notes.—Marr, D. G. Introduction.—Ho Chi Minh. Prison diary.—Marr, D. G. Introduction.
1. Phan Boi Chau. 2. Ho Chi Minh, 1890-1969. 3. Political prisoners—China—Biography. 4. Political prisoners—Vietnam—Biography. I. Jenkins, Christopher. II. Tran Khanh Tuyet. III. Huynh Sanh Thong. IV. Marr, David G. V. Phan Boi Chau. Nguc trung thu. English. 1978. VI. Ho Chi Minh, 1890-1969. Nhat ky trong tu. English. 1978. VII. Series: Southeast Asia Regional Council. Translations Project Group series ; v. 1.

DS556.83.P46A3313   959.7'03'0922   78-1369
ISBN 0-8214-0375-3
ISBN 0-8214-0386-9 pbk.

Copyright © 1978 by Ohio University Press
All rights reserved

Printed in the United States of America
by Oberlin Printing Company, Oberlin, Ohio

CONTENTS

Foreword	vii
Preface to the Book	ix

Phan Boi Chau's *Prison Notes*

Introduction by David G. Marr		3

Prison Notes

I.	Why did Lung Chi-kuang throw me in jail?	9
II.	I was born after we had lost the south for six years	10
III.	Together with my comrades we organize a group of Can Vuong scholars	11
IV.	We want to attack the city of Nghe An	13
V.	Cuong De becomes our titular leader	14
VI.	We visit Hoang Hoa Tham and then go south	17
VII.	*Ryuku's Bitter Tears*	19
VIII.	How can we buy weapons?	21
IX.	I escape to China and meet Nguyen [Thien] Thuat and Liu Yung-fu in Canton	25
X.	I meet Liang Ch'i-ch'ao and Inukai Tsuyoshi	28
XI.	Taking Cuong De abroad	32
XII.	I appeal to the youth to go to Japan to study	36
XIII.	I meet Hoang Hoa Tham	39
XIV.	The Provisional Government of New Vietnam	42
XV.	We want to transport weapons back to help Hoang Hoa Tham	45
XVI.	Ch'en Ch'i-mei and Hu Han-min help us	49
XVII.	Lung Chi-kuang throws me in jail	52

Ho Chi Minh's *Prison Diary*
    Introduction by David G. Marr   59
    Prison Diary   67
Notes   99
Index   111

FOREWORD

The Translations Project Group is engaged in sponsoring translations of Southeast Asian source materials. Formed in late 1970 as a subcommittee of the Southeast Asia Regional Council's Research Committee, the Group endeavors to respond to the need for translations of important works from Southeast Asian languages. The Group decided that initial translation efforts into English should focus on materials of a biographical nature emanating from the various countries of Southeast Asia. The Group sponsored two previous works, *Indonesia Accuses* (translated and edited by Roger Paget) and *The Voyages of Mohamed Ibrahim Munshi* (translated and edited by Amin Sweeney and Nigel Phillips), published by the Oxford University Press. The next volume being produced by the Ohio University Press is *Carving the Path to the Summit* by Ahmad Boestamam, edited and translated by William Roff.

The members of the Translations Project Group wish to express their appreciation to the Southeast Asia Council and its parent organization, the Association for Asian Studies, for facilitating its efforts and to the Ford Foundation for providing the necessary funds.

Dr. Paul W. van der Veur (Chairperson), Professor of Political Science, Ohio University

Dr. Charles Houston, Associate Professor of History, Western Michigan University

Dr. David Marr, Research School of Pacific Studies, Australian National University

Mr. John Musgrave, Southeast Asian Bibliographer, University of Michigan

Dr. William Roff, Professor of History, Columbia University

Dr. David Wyatt, Associate Professor of History, Cornell University

PREFACE TO THE BOOK

After more than a century of French, Japanese and American intervention, Vietnamese can once again breathe the fresh air of independence. That this is true is due in no small measure to the efforts of the two men whose writings are translated here. Phan Boi Chau took a leading role in turning people's minds away from archaic political formulations and away from self-pity over being defeated by the French. He demanded that people look outwards, that they find new solutions for themselves and, above all, that they not allow the French to convince them that they were inferior or in need of colonial tutelage. It was a difficult, indeed dangerous, position to maintain in early twentieth-century Vietnam.

Ho Chi Minh picked up where Phan Boi Chau left off, travelling extensively to see things for himself, analysing French strengths and weaknesses first hand. He turned to Marxism-Leninism as the best available explanation of what was happening in both the world at large and in his own small country of Vietnam. He joined the Comintern because he had come to believe in the solidarity of oppressed peoples and because the Comintern was at the time the most effective international network for counterattacking colonialism. Whereas Phan Boi Chau's vision had remained limited mostly to East Asia, Ho Chi Minh understood the relationship of events in Paris, London, Moscow, New York, Algiers, and New Delhi to those in Vietnam. His special gift was being both internationalist and firmly patriotic.

Many Vietnamese anticolonialists died for their beliefs. Almost all of those active before 1945 spent at least some time in jail; indeed, the French colonial prisons were often referred to not inaccurately as "graduate schools of revolution."[1] There was something of a tradition of jail literature in China, and Vietnamese literature too had similar precedents.[2] Given the nature of prison existence and the meager amount of news filtering in from the world outside, well-educated Vietnamese like Phan Boi Chau or Ho Chi Minh often resorted to poetry, short essays or contemplative diaries to pass the time productively. During the same years—1914-1917—that Phan was languishing in a Canton jail, many of his scholar contemporaries were trying to survive the heat and foul environs of Con Son Prison by composing and reciting poems to each other. While Ho Chi Minh was being shoved from one Kwangsi jail to another in 1942 and 1943, many of his comrades were organizing study sessions inside the overflowing prisons of Hanoi, Son Tay, Lao Bao, Kontum, Con Son, and Chi Hoa (Saigon). The works of one generation were passed on successfully to the next generation; and when these patriots too were thrown into jail the tradition was continued and enriched.

Thus, the creations of Phan Boi Chau and Ho Chi Minh translated here are only two of hundreds of examples of prison literature emerging from the Vietnamese revolution. In more recent years letters, poems and essays of vigor and stunning imagery continued to be written and smuggled out by the tens of thousands of Vietnamese held in prison by the Thieu regime, right up until the last days of April 1975.[3] Phan Boi Chau would probably have died less troubled if he could somehow have looked ahead and seen these men and women refusing to bow, keeping up the struggle no matter what the cost. Ho Chi Minh died in 1969 when hundreds of thousands of American troops still occupied a sizable segment of his country. Yet it seems clear from a brief will and testament penned only months before that he was sure of victory, certain that his life had been meaningful. As readers proceed mentally to enter the cells along with Phan Boi Chau and Ho Chi Minh and share their inner thoughts, they might ask how they themselves would have reacted in similar situations. While there are probably no easy answers, the questioning is worth the effort.

Prison Notes

INTRODUCTION to Phan Boi Chau's *Prison Notes*

PHAN BOI CHAU is revered today as a Vietnamese patriot of the first order. Streets are named after him in all parts of Vietnam. His birthplace in Nghe An province is a national monument. His writings—at least those that managed to survive colonial proscription and confiscation—are now published widely, analysed minutely, and incorporated in university and secondary school curricula. Several poems by Phan Boi Chau are remembered and recited eagerly by Vietnamese of all ages and backgrounds. His name is synonymous with tough, unyielding resistance to foreign domination.

Yet when Phan died in 1940, he was convinced that he had accomplished very little. For all the public adulation, both today and when he was alive, Phan was a self-confessed failure in almost everything he did. As a youth he helped organize a group to oppose the first French troops entering his home province, only to see them dispersed "like a flock of birds." His family house was destroyed, his father stricken. Later he tried to smuggle a large shipment of modern rifles into Indochina, but ran afoul of Chinese merchants' avarice and British customs agents. Even more ambitiously, he attempted to involve Japan on the side of Vietnamese patriots struggling against the French, only to watch in dismay and bitterness as Tokyo and Paris signed an agreement recognizing each other's colonial possessions and subsequently proceeded to cooperate in hounding Vietnamese and Korean anticolonial émigrés from one location to another.

During this period Phan Boi Chau did succeed in constructing a covert anticolonial apparatus of unprecedented scope, but he then was forced to stand by helplessly as the French armed forces and secret police struck back sharply, killing or imprisoning most of his closest comrades and finally smashing the organization. Following the 1911 Revolution in China there was another upsurge of hope and action, with Phan in particular pleading with his Kuomintang friends for some sort of anti-imperialist coalition. But the Kuomintang leaders were having ample troubles of their own and were not even able to protect the Vietnamese émigrés from retaliation. Thus it was that Phan found himself being tossed unceremoniously into a Canton jail by a warlord opponent of the Kuomintang. It was at this point, in early 1914, that Phan wrote *Nguc Trung Thu* (*Prison Notes*), the autobiography translated here.

After his release in 1917 Phan tried hard once again, but wherever he went in China he seemed to be treated as an impoverished scholar, a quaint if respectable émigré pensioner. Nevertheless, the French secret police continued to follow Phan's activities. Eventually they thought him important enough to kidnap him in Shanghai, spirit him to Hanoi, and put him on trial for his life. There were mass demonstrations and outspoken press criticism as a result, however, leading the Governor-General to soften the punishment. Phan was allowed to live out his remaining years in a small, constantly guarded house in the central Vietnamese city of Hue.[1]

As indicated above, *Nguc Trung Thu* was written in early 1914 just after entering that Canton jail. For the author this incident was a terrible setback, a low-point in a life seemingly filled with low-points. Phan wrote *Nguc Trung Thu* hastily, for he had reason to fear that his captor, Governor Lung Chi-kuang, would soon negotiate his transfer to French custody in exchange for certain favors along the Yunnan-Hanoi railway. If this happened, Phan probably faced summary execution since a French colonial court had passed the death sentence *in absentia* on him just the preceding year.

Because this missive, written in classical Chinese, might well be his last, Phan treated it as something of a final testament to his fellow countrymen, both a passionate statement of anti-colonial purpose and a touching apology for not having done better. He included a fair amount of detail on his life as a young man before 1900 (Phan had been born in 1867). And, throughout, Phan tried to expose his individual outlook, his overall attitude and response to events.

Such attention to personal upbringing and psychological motivation was unprecedented in the history of Vietnamese letters. In this Phan may have been influenced by his reading of Western biographical material (in Chinese translation), or by Liang Ch'i-ch'ao's well-known study of Mazzini, Garibaldi, and Cavour. However, of even greater importance was the fact that Phan, a sensitive, proud, intelligent member of the Vietnamese scholar élite, had been deeply, irretrievably shaken by the loss of Vietnam to France and the élite's complete inability to lead an effective counterattack. This trauma had caused many other scholars to retreat to their home villages and the solace of wine, idle poetry and the residual respect of the unlettered towards the lettered. Still others actively joined the French.

For an important minority, however, such profoundly shocking developments were the occasion not for retreat or collaboration but rather a severe, searching reappraisal of Vietnam's position in the world. As might be expected, this soon led to a reassessment of traditional wisdom in light of modern concepts and scientific advances—all with an eye to regaining freedom and independence for their small country. Phan Boi Chau was one of those most deeply engaged in this process, although he preferred to think of himself as an activist, a leader of men engaged in planning and implementing the rapid overthrow of colonial rule. Thus, *Nguc Trung Thu* is first and foremost a revealing chronology of the author's personal introduction to the outside world, and his maturing intellectual and political responses during the most important decade of his life (1903-1913).[2]

Within weeks of his incarceration, Phan apparently smuggled the *Nguc Trung Thu* manuscript out via a sympathetic Chinese prison cook. Associates patiently penned duplicates, so that eventually copies were available in Vietnam and throughout East Asia. A Japanese translation was available a decade or so later and was republished just prior to World War II.[3] Inside Vietnam, however, *Nguc Trung Thu* was not able to circulate as widely as Phan's previous works since the French *Sûreté* had expanded and improved greatly on its apparatus of surveillance and confiscation. As far as can be ascertained, it was not until 1950 that a locally published version (in *quoc ngu*, or romanized script) was made available to the Vietnamese reading public.[4]

What, then, is the long-term significance of *Nguc Trung Thu*? In the first instance, the work is a relatively straightforward narrative autobiography, invaluable in following Phan Boi Chau's hectic operations against the French prior to 1914 and in beginning to understand the basic attitudes of his contemporary group. Here it must be read in conjunction with a second, longer autobiographical effort by Phan, the *Nien Bieu* (*Year to Year Activities*) written around 1937 and recently translated into French by Georges Boudarel.[5] In actuality, the *Nien Bieu* is more reflective, more carefully organized, more consistent and substantial in content. Nevertheless, as a document for historical analysis it may be said to represent a less precise reflection of the author's earlier predisposition for angry, passionate activist involvement than *Nguc Trung Thu*. Both efforts are overtly didactic in tone, designed largely to urge his fellow countrymen onward, while encouraging them to avoid some of his major errors and misconceptions.

In short, each autobiography needs to be read with an understanding of conditions prevailing at the time of writing. In 1914 Phan was forty-seven and—if he survived—still ready and eager to lead the anticolonial struggle. When he was finally released in 1917, as a result of Lung Chi-kuang's military reversals, Phan immediately rejoined some of his comrades in Shanghai, travelled to Japan to test the political climate there, jumped back to Peking to make contact with the German consulate, and then started a long, dangerous and roundabout trip back to Vietnam. While walking through Kweichow province, however, Phan read with deep dismay of the November 1918 armistice in Europe. His plans, such as they were, had been premised on the war's continuing for several years. Demoralized and penniless, Phan made his way back to Hangchow. He would keep struggling, somehow, until he was shipped from Shanghai to Hanoi to await his trial and punishment in 1924.

In 1937, on the other hand, Phan was seventy years old, physically and emotionally exhausted, and highly conscious of the fact that a younger anticolonial generation was moving ahead vigorously with only occasional attention to what he, a battered if not beaten member of the scholar-gentry, had to say.

He did try to cooperate discreetly with his old friend Huynh Thuc Khang, who had emerged from Con Son (Poulo Condore) prison in 1921 and eventually been permitted to establish a popular *quoc-ngu* newspaper in Hue. Phan Boi Chau died three years after completing the *Nien Bieu*, still refusing collaboration with the French, still cultivating the austere simplicity so favored by revolutionary figures, traditional and modern.

Beyond strictly autobiographical content, however, *Nguc Trung Thu* has a special literary quality that will always recommend it to Vietnamese readers. As one commentator has stated, Phan Boi Chau put "all his blood and tears" into this work.[6] This is reflected in the high proportion of warm colloquial imagery, the strikingly appropriate metaphors taken from classical texts (which Phan naturally knew by heart), and the relative avoidance of flowery rhetoric and artificial parallelisms so characteristic of Chinese writing prior to the early twentieth century. Indeed, in this work as well as others, Phan was an early pathfinder in the effort to break away from the involuted hyperbole of the past, cutting modifiers, shortening sentences, and incorporating popular spoken terminology wherever possible. This in turn had an influence on the burgeoning *quoc-ngu* literature of the 1920s and 1930s.

All of this is not to say that *Nguc Trung Thu* is the easiest work of prose for Vietnamese to read today. Some of the stylistic trends that Phan Boi Chau helped initiate proceeded far beyond what he might have anticipated. Other influences played a role later on, so that the Vietnamese language, both spoken and written, has continued to grow and to change with amazing speed. Recognizing these developments, Christopher Jenkins and Tran Khanh Tuyet, the translators of this work, have attempted to capture much of the spirit of the earlier literary form without making it sound too stilted and quaint to the English-language reader. Always they have tried to remain faithful to the original text while hoping not to distract the reader unnecessarily or upset his sense of proper English.

In rendering Vietnamese names each portion of the name has been capitalized and hyphens excluded. Many of the names with diacritical marks can be found in the glossary to my earlier work.⁷ The name for the country is treated as Vietnam, except in romanized renderings of Vietnamese proper names in which it is Viet-Nam.

D.G.M.

Phan Boi Chau

PRISON NOTES

I. WHY DID LUNG CHI-KUANG THROW ME IN JAIL?

A bird about to die sings a sorrowful song; a man about to die speaks righteous words. Whether the words I speak here be righteous or not, I do not know. I only know that they are the words of a man about to die.

In the winter of the year of the Buffalo [1913] I was staying at Duong Thanh when the French Governor-General of Indochina[1] came to Canton. He carried with him warrants for the arrest of the revolutionary leaders of Vietnam asking the Kwangtung government to detain them and hand them over to the French for punishment.

The present Governor of Kwangtung, Lung Chi-kuang, agreed to the request and threw me into jail on the eighth day before the end of the year and told me that sooner or later he would turn me over to the French.

I know that one of these days my head will be chopped off, yet I manage to keep my spirits high. Alas! How many years have I been running around plotting a hundred things without achieving a single one? I am one who bears heavy guilt and many faults—what happiness remains that I should want to go on living?

But before I die why not utter a few sorrowful words before the very end. Who knows my heart? Who says I am guilty? Until the last minute before they bury me under the ground I shall still be trying to dry up this stream of words. A lonely shadow abandoned to the world, a lamplight flickering in the wind and rain, I gather together the history of my life, shedding the tears I have withheld these tens of years—tears with which, mixed in my blood, I write this book. Oh, my thirty million beloved countrymen,[2] whether or not you know my heart, whether or not you hold me guilty, when you read this book you will see my blood nearly dry, yet still wet, upon the page.

II. I WAS BORN AFTER WE HAD LOST THE SOUTH
     FOR SIX YEARS

In the fifteenth year of the reign of King Tu Duc, in the year of the Dog [1862], French soldiers occupied the southern part of our country.

The south is the natural treasure of our country; Saigon, a gateway to the sea, is our very throat. Now it had fallen into the hands of the French. We had not yet lost the whole country, but it was to be just a matter of time. The golden bowl had been overturned, the country almost lost. What a pity for me to be born at that time.

To be more precise, I was born during the year of the Cat in the twentieth year of the reign of Tu Duc [1867], in other words, a full six years after the South had been lost.[3] I was really too young to know anything, still tied to my mother. Yet the seas wept and the mountains cried out in a tragedy that was preparing to drag me into one of its sorrowful acts. That creature in the vast blue heavens, who could it be?[4]

At the beginning of the eighteenth century a new wave of Western learning that was to have far-reaching consequences gushed forth;[5] the echoes of its power and prosperity were ringing in nearly every corner of the globe. If I had been born at that time perhaps I would not have been so blind and stupid as I am today. But alas, I have been unlucky enough to be born into the Vietnam of today.

Formerly our country was dependent on China—we have been part of its territory, we have shared its history and origins for thousands of years as two long-time brother countries. And for this reason our country worships Chinese scholarship, as if it were a holy spirit. But in Chinese studies only literary examinations are considered important.

From the time I was small until I was grown up I have always had a certain native intelligence, studied painstakingly, and worked hard and efficiently. Yet, in terms of accomplishment, I did nothing more than engage in a simple quest for success in the civil examinations.

At that time, the T'ang method of examination preparation[6] was a vogue sought after as the wind chases clouds in a storm. Our people pursued this shadow fearing only that they might fail to imitate exactly the Chinese. Our people wanted to ride the clouds and fly with the wind; for them it was impossible not to follow the way of the examination. And whether or not they wanted to follow this fashion, there seemed no other way to follow.

Alas! The broom in our house was worn out, yet still we thought it precious; that which we come to like over time becomes a habit. And so I too was tied to fashion, to such a degree that I wasted so many days and months following a destiny of examination preparation for almost half a man's lifetime. That indeed must be judged a very large stain upon my life.

III. TOGETHER WITH MY COMRADES WE ORGANIZE A GROUP OF CAN VUONG SCHOLARS[7]

When I was seventeen, in the thirty-sixth year of the reign of Tu Duc, the year of the Goat [1883], the French seized Hanoi and the provinces of Bac Ky.[8] And by the time I was nineteen, the year of the Cock [1885], in the first year of the reign of Ham Nghi, the French had invaded the capital of Hue and King Ham Nghi was forced to flee. The royal palace presented a desolate scene; flocks of deer frolicked while crows made their nests. And so, in the seventh month of the first year of the reign of Ham Nghi, began the tragedy of losing our country. Alas! The sky was falling and the earth shook! In such times what man that walks the earth and lives beneath the sky could look upon his country with eyes of wood and stone, in indifference and resignation?

Fate endowed me with an incredibly quick temper. From the days when I was but a small child I read the books that our ancestors had handed down to us and every time I read the stories of how our ancestors were so eager to die for the righteous cause, I soaked the book with a flood of tears. I often used to remember and talk about such meritorious officials as Truong Cong Dinh[9] who died in the loss of Nam Ky[10] and Nguyen Tri Phuong[11] who committed suicide in Hanoi. But every time I was reminded of them I shook my fist and beat my breast, ashamed of myself that I was so far behind these two men. It was simply my nature and I could not pretend to be otherwise.

After the loss of the capital, King Ham Nghi was brought in the royal carriage to a mountain stronghold in the province of Ha Tinh. All the notables and officials who withdrew to their home districts, such as Nguyen Xuan On[12] and Dinh Van Chat,[13] vied among themselves to be the first to raise the flag of rebellion in support of the king. The Can Vuong movement spread to all districts and provinces. As I look back, I realize that I was but a young school boy. What power could I have had to dare join the elders in mounting an uprising? I was like a small bird whose wings are not yet fully feathered, with fangs and claws still weak. Oh what a sorry state! I thought of the heroic story of Dong Thien Vuong[14] who at the age of three rode a horse into battle. And I thought that surely I must be a cowardly little boy.

Tossing things back and forth in my mind, searching for a solution, the best I could come up with was an appeal to my fellow classmates to organize a company of schoolboys to help the King. We called it the Si Tu Can Vuong Doi [Scholar's Unit to Protect the King]. I and my good friend Tran Van Luong were the founders. The honorable licenciate Dinh Xuan Sung[15] was our commander. I was the lieutenant commander. Our group numbered a little over one hundred men.

We were quite well organized although we had not yet found any way to obtain weapons or supplies. Meanwhile the French had brought many troops to level the city of Nghe An and then went on to wipe out many other districts and provinces. Our company with neither financial support nor guns and ammunition was scattered and dispersed in a very short time like a flock of birds. In order to escape I was forced to flee and hide myself among the refugees.

When I think back to what we did at that time, it was no different from a group of children playing with paper houses. No wonder the scholars laughed at us. Nevertheless, I write down these experiences because they were my heart's budding schemes to save the country. Although I might have engaged in a game of self-deception, by nature my heart is honest. And so I will not indulge in hiding my weaknesses.

By this time the house of my family had been destroyed by the fighting, and my father, besieged by misfortune, had become gravely ill. My mother had passed away and I had no brothers and sisters. Therefore, I dared not leave my father or direct my attention to any other task. I resigned myself to take refuge at home where for a total of nine years I taught school and, of course, took care of my father.

IV. WE WANT TO ATTACK THE CITY OF NGHE AN

But during those nine years I devoted much time to carefully preening my wings so one day I might be able to step forth strongly into the struggle. It was my habit to come together with my comrades to plot and scheme. We joined the group led by Vuong Thuc Quy (whose father led his village guard in a nationalist revolt against the Protectorate government and was killed) or that of Ha Van My (a veteran follower of Phan Dinh Phung,[16] who was later arrested by the Protectorate government and then committed suicide). Every year on the anniversary of the founding of the French republic[17] we met secretly with our fellow accomplices in the city of Nghe-An to plot our attack. But the forces of the Protectorate were too numerous and their defences were too solid. We could not succeed. There remains the fact, however, that during these occasions we adventurous knights were able to get to know each other and to establish links among ourselves. Such was the beginning that was to guide my activities in the years after.

When I was thirty or so the Can Vuong groups all over the country broke up and dispersed. The only one who remained was Phan Dinh Phung in La Son[18] who tried to carry on his resistance a while longer. But in the year of the Horse, the sixth year of the reign of Thanh Thai [1894] Phan Dinh Phung died. From that time on the country seemed deserted and melancholy. There was no one left to shoulder the responsibility. For some ten years I bore anger in my heart and nourished a great ambition to raise the flag of independence in the area between Hong mountain and Lam river.[19] I could no longer hold myself back from acting.

Thus, I was born and reared in a barbaric situation, and all I knew to do with my time was wander aimlessly in a forest of literary exams. To speak of our scholarship in relation to that available in Europe, there is no comparison. Yet, our scholarship did promote and teach the meaning of decency; I refused to play servant or follow the ass of anyone. At that time the old Can Vuong groups had breathed their last breath, while new groups had not yet blossomed forth. For a long time I went to meetings and, in fact, became more well known in society than before. I thought especially at that time that if I did not engage in action, then who would? Whatever my accomplishments up to now, they are due to such deep reflection and meditation.

Nevertheless, how stupid could I have been? In view of the considerable strength of the French on the one hand and the pettiness of my own capabilities on the other, I relied on the people. Yet the people were still at a low level of political awareness. I counted on the times to be favorable but we fell upon hard times, that goes without saying. I was not cautious but relied on my inflexible temper. I had hoped to patch up the sky and to fill in the ocean—who dares say that I wasn't crazy! And so I marched on enthusiastically, throwing caution to the winds. Could there have been anyone on this earth more stupid than myself?

V. CUONG DE BECOMES OUR TITULAR LEADER

I began to attempt to bring together a brave band of brigands and all those left over from the Can Vuong movement to raise the flag of national revolt in the Nghe-Tinh area. And so for a while there were many who came to drink and swap tales and we grew to be close friends.

The old followers of Phan Dinh Phung, such as Quynh Quang, the followers of Bach Xi, and the group of Kiem and Cong used to come to my home all the time.[21]

My house was used as a school, but the students only came to the house in front while in the house behind we harbored many heroic fugitives. The old scholars in the village who passed by were startled when they glanced in and saw such a state of affairs. Shaking their heads and clucking their tongues, they never again dared peek into my house.

Our strategy firmed up as the day drew near when we were to meet together to launch our uprising.

But my close friend Dang Thai Than[22] said to me: "As I look back on the circumstances of our situation we have not yet had an opportunity to engage in any large action. If we continue to hurry along carelessly, surely we will accomplish nothing. Yet we must find a way to show the French that our people are not all cowards. It is fine to affront danger once. But I hope that once we raise our voices there will be someone who will continue to carry on afterwards.

"If we begin the struggle only in the Nghe-Tinh area, I am afraid that it will be like a fetus that is difficult to bear which, once squeezed from its mother's womb, dies before uttering a cry. It is for these reasons that I worry for you.

"I think first of all we should go from north to south appealing to our heroic brothers in both places to join together to work with us. In the north there are many righteous men, and from Quang Nam southward we are not lacking men of chivalry. Once harmony has been established with them, all of us from all three areas can rise up simultaneously to divide and weaken the strength of the enemy. With the support of numerous accomplices perhaps our work will have some results."

Dang Thai Than was a courageous man of enthusiastic nature, with a great sense of human dignity. For ten years he was both my teacher and my friend. And now as I listened to his words of great wisdom I felt awakened. Immediately I made plans to go from north to south to bring together all groups and factions from all over the country and arrange for an uprising in the future.

Dang Van Ba,[23] a friend of my own age, agreed with the decision I had made and together we set out for the south.

As I went south this time I heard that in the Can Vuong group of Quang Nam and Quang Ngai provinces there was a veteran leader named Nguyen Thanh,[24] who, after being arrested, was fortunate enough to be pardoned with the help of Nguyen Than.[25] He was said to be living now in the mountains with all the intense energy of former days. The fire of his will had not gone out, the cinders were still burning. He was like a bird awaiting the autumn wind.

In the second month of the year of the Cat [1903] during the spring, I went to Quang Nam with Dang Thai Than and Dang Van Ba. As we passed through Hue we met Le Vo[26] who had returned from Binh Dinh.

He came from a family of generals. Four of his brothers had died in service to the country. He was the youngest in the family and therefore was lucky enough to still be alive. When I met him in the capital he displayed such will as to lay out before me the very bile from his liver. We spent day and night together and became intimate friends. He joined us as we set out for Quang Nam in search of Nguyen Thanh.

This man, a leader of the nationalist uprising when only eighteen years old, fought with great vehemence and often forced the enemy into defeat. Even the enemy was forced to admire the way in which he commanded his troops. He was unsurpassed among our righteous forces.

When we arrived we introduced ourselves to each other. But it seemed as if we had actually been good friends since long ago. As we gathered around him to drink and talk together, Nguyen Thanh discussed our common task forcefully and in a clear, righteous manner.

I brought up my idea and started to explain it. "Excellent!" he exclaimed as he clapped his hands together. "Whoever wants to devise a scheme now for our great cause has first of all to fulfill these three conditions: first, he must win the heart of the people; second, he must collect a large sum of money; and third, he must supply and arm our troops sufficiently. Once we have won people's confidence we will be able to collect a large sum of money. And once we have money the problem of weapons will not be difficult to solve at all.

"But we must understand the customs and the level of understanding of our people—we cannot imitate European ways. We are looking for a way to appeal effectively to the people's hearts.

If we do not speak in terms of supporting the monarchy, then the large and wealthy families will not follow us. And although we may have the sincerest intention of saving the country, if we do not support the monarchy we will die only to prove our patriotism to ourselves, while in fact our death will have been in vain towards the achievement of any larger task.

"King Ham Nghi is wandering somewhere far off.[27] For a long time we have had no news of him. And King Thanh Thai is now under French control, and there is no way that we might bring him close to us. A descendant of the virtuous Crown Prince Canh, the first son of Cao Hoang,[28] is still living and available to us at this time. As we begin our rebellion we should, before anything else, respectfully ask him to govern the palace. Only in this way will our name be accepted, our orders passed on. Every time we raise our voices and cry out, certainly our words will be carried by the favorable wind and will echo and resound for great distances. What do you all think?"

I and Dang Thai Than and Dang Van Ba and Le Vo actually had never thought of honoring a member of the royal family in such a way. But now, listening to Nguyen Thanh, we thought it very reasonable.

Alas! The intellectual standard of the people had not yet been developed; we had not given up our old ways. As we moved from family loyalties to nationalism, we might have wished that the people would throw out the ancient ways and sweep the slate clean, but it was not so easy. After listening to the words that Nguyen Thanh had just spoken, I could only submit myself to them.

VI. WE VISIT HOANG HOA THAM AND THEN GO SOUTH

In the third month of the year of the Cat [1903] I visited Prince Cuong De in Hue and explained to him our project.[29]

The Prince answered cheerfully: "For a long time I have nourished that great ideal. From the time my two dear friends, Ho Quy Chau and Nguyen Thu Nam, passed away it has been my misfortune to search far and wide for someone with whom I might discuss these affairs. But I have found no one. Now you will not fail to set out on this long journey with courage. We have confidence in each other's integrity. I will be happy to sacrifice everything to have this one chance out of ten thousand to show my gratitude to the country. Even though I be forced to lie down on thorns or swallow bitter bile—even though my body be torn in pieces and disappear—this also shall be my happiness."

Then the Prince together with Le and Dang and myself went south to Quang Nam and gathered together all of our comrades at the mountain retreat of Nguyen Thanh.

We discussed our work in secret and together honored the Prince as the leader of our group. We distributed the responsibility for the work of the group, putting Nguyen Thanh in charge of the region from the two provinces of Quang Nam and Quang Ngai on down to the south, while I assumed responsibility for the area from Quang Binh and Quang Tri on up to the north.

In the sixth month of that year[30] I returned to Nghe An and then set out almost immediately for the north. I wandered through more than ten provinces setting up the project of our group and seeking out supporters.

Finally, after a difficult climb into the mountains, I arrived in the area of Yen The and came to the outpost of Phon Xuong in order to visit the exalted Hoang Hoa Tham.[31]

Hoang Hoa Tham was probably the toughest among the old Can Vuong group surviving in the north. From the time Nguyen Bich[32] had been killed in battle and Nguyen Thien Thuat[33] had fled to China the Can Vuong movement in the north had faded and dispersed. Over ten years before, Hoang Hoa Tham by himself had invaded the mountainous area of Bac Giang in order to resist the Protectorate. The French gave this part of the forest to him to administer in order to make peace with him. Among all the people in our country—even among the women and children—there was no one who hadn't heard of the fame and reputation of Hoang Hoa Tham.

This was the first time that I had set foot in this outpost. I remember that day was the eighth day of the eighth month of the year of the Cat [1903]. Two men came with me on the trip, Nguyen Cu[34] and Nguyen Dien.[35] These two men waited outside the outpost. I alone went inside.

I was unlucky enough to arrive at a time when Hoang Hoa Tham was seriously ill. There was no way that I could meet with him. But he ordered his eldest son, Ca Trong, and two beloved lieutenants, Ca Dinh and Ca Huynh, to provide a warm and kind welcome for me.

I stayed at the outpost for eleven days, not leaving until I had revealed in confidence all my deepest thoughts.

From that time on the movement in the North was organized once again.

In the tenth month I returned to Hue and reported to Prince Cuong De about my work. He said to me:

"The southern area was originally opened up and developed by the Nguyen family. Profiting from this, the virtuous Gia Long brought about a stunning restoration of the old kingdom. We long for those old days very much. You should take a trip to the south. I'm sure your trip will have a strong influence."

And so in the middle of the twelfth month of the year of the Cat [1904] I set out for the south.

At the end of the twelfth month my boat arrived in Saigon. During the first month of the year of the Dragon [1904] I went to Chau Doc and Ha Tien looking for talented and heroic men in the Seven Mountains area.[36] I wandered all over the provinces of Can Tho, Vinh Long and Sa Dec. I took this occasion to visit the places which still bore the stamp of Nguyen Huan[37] and Truong Cong Dinh in the hope that something interesting might turn up.

But on this trip I found little of great interest. In truth, I had expected more . . .[38]

VII. *Ryuku's Bitter Tears*

In the third month of the year of the Dragon [1904] I returned from the south to Hue. From time to time I thought of ways to add feet to our dragon. This was an important event in my life and warrants some discussion.

At the time King Dong Khanh ascended the throne, France and Vietnam modified the conditions of their treaty.[39] The land from Thanh Hoa south to Binh Thuan was made a French

Protectorate and called Annam. The keys to the door of the Protectorate Government were held tightly in the fist of the French *Résident Supérieur*. All real power over military and financial affairs was held by the French, while administrative positions were left to our people. The French oversaw and commanded the work.

I felt that if a group of people within the officialdom would help us in secret, certainly our work would be easier. But when I thought it over I realized that those in the officialdom were of only common intelligence, and I was afraid that it would be difficult to work with them. If our plotting with them were to be discovered, it would result in immediate disaster for us.

Nevertheless, in spite of my misgivings, we were people who were determined to sacrifice our lives to save the country. Our necks, our lives, we would sacrifice anything—we didn't care. And so we threw ourselves onto the road that might lead to happiness or misfortune. Why should we hesitate and hide any more?

Thus, I decided to look for a way to motivate the officials. At that time I was well-known in the capital as a literary figure[40] and most of the important elders in the court wanted me to become one of their followers.

Right away I wrote a book called *Luu Cau Huyet Le Tan Thu* [*Ryuku's Bitter Tears*]. In the book I described clearly the distressing sight of the disintegration of the capital, the loss of the country and the shame of lords who have become servants. I talked about how it was urgent to develop the intellectual standards of the people and nourish the popular zeal in order to build a foundation for the task of saving the country, etc. . . . The book was several thousand characters long.

I brought some copies of the book to show to important elders such as the Minister of the Eastern Chambers[41] Nguyen Thang, Public Works Minister Dao Tien, Minister of Rites Ho Le, Minister of the Interior Nguyen Thuat, etc. . . .

The elders admired my tough words and literary style and secretly admitted that my ideas were correct, but all the while they dared not speak straightforwardly of their own ideas.

Wandering aimlessly these long months I finally understood

that I could not rely on the elders at all. In their gut they only knew how to seek wealth and honors for themselves and their families. When they saw that something was about to happen, they would merely sit and watch to see whether it was a success or a failure. And then afterwards they would choose their allegiances according to which direction the winds of fortune had blown. Now we had opened ourselves to danger by confiding in them. Surely we could not rely on them in any way. I was ashamed of myself that I was weak in spirit and dullwitted. I had not the talent to make a marble statue nod its head.[42] The more I think the more I regret that I had dreamt of taking advantage of the officials. Surely that was nonsense.

But this effort was not without results.

After *Ryuku's Bitter Tears* appeared, various individual patriots passing their time inconspicuously in the capital understood clearly what my feelings were. Men such as Phan Chau Trinh[43] and Tran Quy Cap,[44] later to be jailed or chopped in half, at this time became my intimate friends thanks principally to my book *Ryuku's Bitter Tears*.

VIII. HOW CAN WE BUY WEAPONS?

Now all brave and righteous people around the country were in contact and with one heart.

From the north down to Hue throughout all important provinces, districts and cities, we had secretly arranged support for our group. We had only to wait for the proper opportunity to begin.

There were also compatriots who had taken on the responsibility of seeking a large sum of money to support our work.

Had I lived during the time of the Dinh, the Ly, the Le or the Trinh,[45] it would have been sufficient merely to raise my arm and cry out a single word and right away the waves would have risen up and the thunder would have echoed and our task would have been achieved in but a short moment.

But these days things are altogether different.

From the time guns and bullets were invented, many weapons such as swords, spears, and knives have become useless. The weapons we used before as sabers or for cutting wood or for fighting the Ch'in and chasing out the Sui[46] nowadays have become totally useless.

We must be aware that the weapons of the French are ten thousand times better than ours. And if ever a gun is carried by one of our men, the high-ranking French officers keep an eye on him day and night. In the ranks of the military none of our men is able to hold a position from corporal on up. To coax our men in the French army to join us and turn their guns against their officers would ordinarily not be an easy affair; unless a great war is produced, perhaps our plots will have been in vain.[47]

All the activists (those specializing in planning strategy) in our group at that time faced an enormously difficult problem that in no way could be solved—the problem of weapons.

In our country there were places that manufactured weapons. But they were all appropriated by the French officers who kept a very close vigil over them. If we just passed by these places and glanced in, right away we were arrested. And so where might we obtain weapons?

It was also impossible to buy weapons abroad and transport them into the country. Every harbor and border post in the country was spied on and investigated extremely carefully by Protectorate authorities. Even if we bought some weapons abroad, we needed a great many, and by what magic power or devilish ruse might we slip them all into the country?

We worried all the time, and were so disorganized that we wasted many days without resolving the problem of weapons. Every time we thought about it everyone felt uneasy and uncomfortable, upset that we were missing what we needed the most. We thought of the old story of Chau Lang who, if he had never had the east wind, could never have fought the battle of Xich-Bich.[48]

Not long after, there was a sudden eruption of gunshots at Port Arthur, in Liaotung [Manchuria], which resounded across the winds and the waves, deafening our ears and making us shake.

The great victory of Japan in the Russo-Japanese war had a

tremendous impact upon us. For it was like a new and strange world opening up.

Before the time of the French Protectorate, Vietnam only knew a world with China. And when the French arrived we only knew a world with France. But the world had changed. A strange new wave as yet undreamed of had arrived.

We had been caught up in our internal affairs for so long that even if our heads were cut off and our bodies lost we still had no fear. We were that way only because we cared for our country and our conscience forced us to be so. As for a way to build independence, at that time we were still dreaming in a very thick fog.

Alas! In the middle of the nineteenth century, even though the universe was shaken by American winds and European rains, our country was still in a period of dreaming in a deep sleep. Our people were still blind and resigned to their lot. We cannot blame them, for even well-known people from the higher classes like myself were like frogs in the bottom of a well or ants at the bottom of their hole. We knew nothing about life. I think that there must be no more tragic-comic people in the world than our people.

It is only because in former times we shut our doors and stayed at home, going round and round in circles of literary knowledge, examinations and Chinese studies. To say frankly that our people were deaf and blind is no exaggeration.

Even after the French invasion our people were still deaf and blind. If we had not been awakened by the violent sound of the guns at Port Arthur, perhaps we should not yet know that there were other foreign countries besides France.

After the beginning of the Russo-Japanese hostilities, during the years of the Dragon [1904] and the Serpent [1905], the competition and struggle between the Europeans and the Asians, between the white-skinned people and the yellow-skinned people, forced us to wake up with a start. We became increasingly enthusiastic and intense in our commitment to our ideals. The only problem we still sought to overcome was that of obtaining weapons.

Towards the end of the tenth month of the year of the Dragon

[1904], all the leaders of the group held an important meeting in Quang Nam province in the mountain village of Nam Thanh. Since this place was close to the capital of Hue, we felt that surely our chairman, Prince Cuong De, would be able to sneak away and come to the meeting.

At that time Tang Bat Ho had just come down from Haiphong, adding another veteran warrior to our ranks. Everyone was extraordinarily happy and enthusiastic.

All the leaders said that without the help of some foreign country the problem of weapons could not be resolved. From the important standpoints of history, geography and race there was no other country that could help us but the Middle Kingdom [China]. But since their defeat at Lang Son[49] in the year of the Monkey [1884] and the signing of the Peking Treaty, China had ceded to France her rights over Vietnam as a tributary state. And in the years of the Cock [1885] and the Dog [1886] following the flight of Ham Nghi, how many of our elders ran to China seeking support, and were not heard from afterward. With these recent examples before us it was useless to place our hope in any help from China.

We discussed with each other the fact that the only country from which we might seek support was Japan. At that time Japan, a yellow-skinned Asian people like ourselves, had just defeated Russia and was becoming a strong power. Perhaps they wanted to be lord and master of all Asia. In any case they would help us if only to weaken the strength of Europe—this would be to their advantage. If we were to go to Japan and tell them our moving story, surely they would assist us. Whether they lent us weapons or helped us to buy them, it wouldn't be difficult.

After some further deliberation everyone decided that we would do as we had discussed. We selected one person to be our plenipotentiary representative to take a letter to Japan from our leader, Prince Cuong De, and see to the problem of weapons.

Needing someone with skill to fill the position of representative, the group unanimously chose me to go to Japan.

IX. I ESCAPE TO CHINA AND MEET NGUYEN [THIEN] THUAT AND LIU YUNG-FU IN CANTON

In obeying the order of our Association,[50] I was leaving the country for the first time.

Although I went principally on this trip as a representative from a particular revolutionary group, I was also the representative of a whole country and her people.

If I were a very talented and intelligent man, if I had been able to study foreign languages, literature, politics and international relations, learning these subjects by heart like those fastidious gentry who memorize every antique and precious item in their home, then, even though I might bear the shame of having lost the country, I would not shy away from the fact that I was as capable as any man on earth. Would this capability not be enough to do honor to our people abroad?

How unfortunate, then, that the first person able to visit the outside world and represent us should be such a stupid and ignorant boor as myself. As for talent, I have none. Outside of three expressions in Chinese, I have not studied properly. Although my head is full of words, it might as well be empty. I am a man who has lost his country. My life is unimportant, and my scholarly credentials are of poor quality. In fact, I have contributed to the degeneration and weakening of our people. But how can I describe it all! What place in this immense universe could put up with me? At night I reflect on myself in secret shame, to the point that my tears flow like blood. And now, as I recall the activities of my former days, I only ask that our people be generous in their judgment of me.

Yet when I was born our land was still immature, our race still ignorant, and we were not yet developed. Even as I crawled from my mother's womb, there was no one to show me the way or to open my mind. It was as if I was locked in chains day and night. People feared only that my eyes might see or my ears hear. Is it any wonder that I was ignorant!

Nevertheless, when I first set out on my mission abroad for the Association, I did not give much thought to this disgrace.

When a bird has been imprisoned in a cage for a long time he longs terribly to see the open sky and the blue clouds. And once he has been able to escape from his cage he is so happy and in such good spirits that he could ride the clouds and fly with the wind. He is in no hurry to think of what he will do afterwards. It was in this way that I set out boldly on my mission.

Towards the end of the twelfth month in the year of the Dragon [1904] I came to the capital [Hue] to have an audience with our titular leader but stayed only long enough to brief him about my mission. Then I visited all the important leaders in our group and discussed our plans with them.

Having completed all final arrangements I set out immediately from Quang Nam on my trip.

Two men accompanied me, Tang Bat Ho and Dang Tu Kinh.

In former days Tang used to be a writer and helped Liu Yung-fu[51] in the planning of his military affairs. He had travelled through Kwangtung, Kwangsi and Taiwan and spoke Cantonese quite fluently.

In the fourth month of that year [1904] Tang had just returned from abroad and together we looked after the affairs of the group. The group made a worthy choice in asking him to accompany me on the trip.

On the second day of the first month in the year of the Serpent [1905] we set out from Haiphong on our trip.

When I got on the boat I spontaneously broke into verse, bidding farewell to my brothers:

> Unusual is the man who would venture forth courageously
> And refuse to allow his fate to be determined by the
>   whirling heavens!
> My job is for one lifetime;
> Future tasks will be taken by those yet to be born.
> The country is lost, we are in the throes of death,
> There are no more righteous scholars, it is useless to study.
> On this ocean I venture along with the wind.
> I see thousands of silver waves dancing in the distance.

From this point on our feet trod on a dangerous road.

The French government did not allow Vietnamese people freedom of movement. Without exception, whoever wanted to go abroad, whether to travel or for business purposes, if he did not have permission from the Protectorate, would surely be accused of secret communication outside the country or of plotting a rebellion. Certainly whoever received permission from the Protectorate to go abroad was a man the French trusted and could rely on—or a man very skillful in persuasion. By nature I had none of these qualifications, and so I was forced to go underground.

Tang had done it many times and knew the way by heart. He showed me the trick of changing my appearance in order to slip across the border.

From Haiphong to Moncay we took a trading boat. I masqueraded as a Chinese businessman, shaving the top of my head and braiding the rest of my hair.

When the boat arrived at the landing we waited until night fall before we dared rent a small fishing boat to go across to Truc Son, Truong Son, which is on the border of Phong Thanh district in China.

Although the trip was dangerous it was an extraordinary delight.

We made it across the border with all our money and important papers intact. Ha! The more strict they grew in trying to control us the more we were able to perfect our techniques for breaking the bars of our cages and escaping from our coops! And it was not just myself—there was to be no shortage of those who would follow my footsteps abroad.

We stayed in Truc Son for a week and then took a sailboat from Kham-Chau for Peihai.

By that time we were well into the second month. But there was quite a strong north-east wind and our boat took only seven days to reach Hiep Pho, where we boarded a British merchant ship for Hong Kong.

When the boat arrived at the wharf we disembarked and wandered around here and there for over a week. In my head I felt a pleasure and happiness that I know not how to describe, while at the same time feeling an equally indescribable suffering.

Since I had fled the country so recently the French were not yet aware of my absence. Once I left their oppression I saw an environment in which everyone was as free as air and could go calmly wherever they pleased. Before, I was no different from a horse locked up in a stable with my eyes sewn shut. Now, it was as if someone had cut the threads. I opened my eyes and ran around, frolicking in the open fields. How wonderful to be free! Yet as I thought of this I remembered the oppression of our people, and I felt as if my bowels had been broken into pieces.

In Hong Kong I saw great numbers of students happily going to school, while the market was bustling day and night; I never saw soldiers stop people in the streets to examine their identification papers; I never saw soldiers nab people walking at night without a lantern and take them to the police station; I never saw that kind of cruel and arrogant patrol that arrests innocent people in the road; and there was no sign of the native people being bullied by the Europeans, forcing them to scurry to the side of the road. Alas! Hong Kong is also a land under the rule of the foreigners, yet there was a springlike feeling of freshness—not as in our country.

At that time I heard that the high-ranking mandarin, Nguyen Thien Thuat, who had earlier fled to Canton because of the loss of the country, was now living in the Liu family temple in Sa-ha. He was a man of the same rank as my father and had participated earlier in the Can Vuong movement. Now that I had arrived here I felt I should speak to him.

I went to Canton to seek him out. When he saw me he was overjoyed and took me to have an audience with Liu Yung-fu.

Liu was now an old man, but as we talked over the old days in Bac Ky, from time to time he pounded the table and let forth a great roar, reminding me of the power he used to display when he fought the French at Cau Giay[52] near Hanoi.

X. I MEET LIANG CH'I-CH'AO[53] AND INUKAI TSUYOSHI[54]

When I came to Canton, Ts'en Ch'un-hsuan was the Governor-General of the two provinces, Kwangtung and Kwangsi.

I sent him a letter[55] explaining clearly how his two provinces and Vietnam in sharing the same border were like lips and teeth;

when lips open in a cry of suffering, the teeth are cold. I reminded him of the feeling between the two countries that had grown intimate through a very long lord-vassal relationship. Then I asked him to help Vietnam in any way possible.

For many days after I sent the letter I received no reply. Perhaps the old man feared the Europeans as if they were tigers. But we were by now familiar with such habits of Manchu officialdom.

We returned to Hong Kong to await the departure of the boat for Japan. However, since the negotiations between Russia and Japan were not yet over, there were no Japanese ships in Hong Kong. Towards the end of the third month I took a commercial boat to Shanghai.

In Shanghai the difficulties of my trip began to appear gradually. The most difficult problem was that of language. I had never studied spoken Chinese or English.

Fortunately all those with whom I came into contact were Chinese. If one knew Chinese characters he could use a brushpen in place of his tongue. But this was extremely inconvenient.

Alas! Being born in this period of the nineteenth and twentieth centuries, one who lacks a good, contemporary education can in no way compete for survival in this world. Language and literature are the paths that lead to learning. It must have been luck that a man as illiterate and boorish as myself had not yet been eliminated from this competition.

Nevertheless, at that time I was forty years old and tied up in the affairs of the Association to the point that I lost my appetite and could not sleep well. Even if I had wanted to take up my books and start studying again for exams as before, I didn't have the time. I counsel all our youth now not to follow the path that I took.

At the beginning of the fourth month I took a Japanese boat from Shanghai, arriving in Yokohama about ten days later. I stayed there for over a week.

When I first went to Japan I did not know a single word of Japanese nor did I have introductions to anyone. Yet, whenever I needed anything I found I could rely on the soldiers who stood guard in the streets. They were very kind in offering me assistance.

I admired very much the procedures of the Japanese police who were organized in such an orderly and proper manner. It made me sad to think of our own police system.

At that time, Liang Ch'i-ch'ao was living in Yokohama, and was editor of *The Renovation of the People* [in Chinese, *Hsin-min ts'ung-bao*]. I had learned that Liang had lived in Japan for a long time and understood Japanese affairs quite well. I decided before anything to go to him and ask him to introduce me to the Japanese.

Although Liang and I had never met each other, I felt that he was a modern, progressive person, a man with thinking eyes, not like the usual lot. I wrote him a letter immediately, asking permission to come and see him. I wrote: 'When we are born we cry out one word and we begin to know and understand each other. But after studying books for ten years we become like members of a family related through marriage.' On this basis of common background I made my request to see Liang.

When he received the letter Liang invited me immediately to call on him. We communicated in brush-writing.[56] Liang asked me why I had come to Japan and then asked me about the situation of the French in Vietnam. I was sorry at that time only to be able to give him a general outline. It was such a long story that I could never have told him everything in just a short brush-stroke conversation.[57]

Soon afterward I wrote *Viet-Nam Vong Quoc Su* [*History of the Loss of Vietnam*] and gave the entire manuscript to Liang to print.[58] This was the first book I had written while out of the country.

After Liang and I had met he treated me with favor and much kindness. And so I explained to him our plan of relying on the Japanese to supply us with weapons so that we might begin our armed insurrection against the French.

Liang said to me: "You have such enthusiasm that I cannot refuse to help you as best I can. Still, I think that from olden days up until now it has not been the custom of foreign countries to aid a revolutionary party to overthrow its government. Such foreign support would only be given in the case that two countries disagree with each other and start to fight. France and

Japan have not yet had the opportunity to fight each other. The Japanese will never agree to supply you with weapons.

"In terms of other means, there are several political parties who might help you on their own, secretly, but this is only a possibility. Among the popular parties at this time in Japan, there is only one that has any power, the Progressive Party,[59] under the leadership of Okuma Shigenobu and Inukai Tsuyoshi. If you would like to meet these two men then I will introduce you to them."

* * * * * *

Afterwards I accompanied Liang to Tokyo to visit Inukai Tsuyoshi. And, in turn, Inukai took us to meet Okuma Shigenobu. From this point on we were able to establish good relations with the Japanese Party.

A few days later Inukai introduced me to all the important figures in his Party.

Fukushima Yasumasa, the chief of staff, and Kashiwabara Buntaro, head of the East Asia Common Culture Society [*Toa Dobun Kai*][60], both welcomed me.

I seized this opportunity immediately to describe to them the ideas for which we were seeking support. They answered:

"Without exception the Japanese people are always happy to aid and support countries of the same continent and race as Japan. But the support that you seek has international implications. Japanese government support will only be possible if we can find a way for them to agree to help secretly. Unfortunately, since the Russian war has just been concluded, my country's government is not yet free to turn its attention to any other task. If you can wait a little while, our Party will try with all its heart to help you. One day we will achieve our ends, do not worry."

They asked me if our Association was monarchical or democratic. I replied:

"The goal of our Association now is above all to force the French to return the right of independence to us. As for monarchy or democracy, that is another problem that we have not yet dealt with. But if we trace the history of our country from early days up until the present time, and if we consider the level of political understanding of the people at this time, then a monarchy would seem to suit us better. For this reason our group has asked Prince Cuong De to become our titular leader. In this way we are preparing for a monarchy in the future."

The Japanese by nature respect their Emperor and support a monarchical form of government. Thus, they felt that what I had said was correct. They said to me:

"If you bring the Prince of your honorable country here, then the alliance of our friendship will grow even stronger. Do you all think so?"

Whether or not I had succeeded in obtaining support, I did not yet know. But I feared that if news of my escape out of the country had spread, something unfortunate might happen to Cuong De. Certainly this would have a great influence on the affairs of our Association. And so I decided to find a way to return to Vietnam and invite Cuong De to leave the country.

XI. TAKING CUONG DE ABROAD

When I first went abroad I tried to focus my attention on the problem of weapons. But during the several months that I spent in Tokyo eating in restaurants and sleeping in hotels I came to understand more clearly the story of the Russo-Japanese war and observe the workings of Japanese politics, education, foreign relations and industry.

To see all this I was terribly ashamed that I had been content before to sit and allow myself to shrivel up within the confines of Vietnam. No wonder my learning was vague and unclear, my thinking deadlocked and empty. Yet all my countrymen and comrades were just like me. What a pity we could not transfer all our people to Japan to expose our brains and eyes to something completely new and different.

After I had decided to bring Cuong De out of the country I realized I had to return to Vietnam. And so in the beginning of the seventh month of the year of the Serpent [1905] I and Dang Tu Kinh took a boat from Yokohama for Vietnam.

I had made this trip to Japan on a mission entrusted to me

by the Association. Yet I left the work only half-completed. Surely I could not avoid the responsibility for this failure.

Nevertheless, there were two tasks I did accomplish that might exculpate me. One was arranging for Cuong De to go abroad, which would strengthen the confidence and commitment of our brothers in Vietnam, while removing Cuong De from any danger that might happen to him if he were to remain in Vietnam.

The second was bringing the tales of all the marvelous new things I had seen and heard back to my compatriots at home. Certainly this would prove useful in making progress towards our modernization in the future. For these two reasons I had no misgivings about returning.

In the eighth month I returned to Haiphong where I stayed with a friend from the Association. It is impossible to describe how happy and relieved I was to be home.

My relief was mostly due to the following. When I arrived in Peihai I ran the risk of taking a French boat, relying on one of the men[61] who stoked the coal to protect me. When the French inspector boarded the boat this man hid me in the very deepest hold and covered me with coal. I lay there in silence, not daring to stir. Thus, escaping detection by the French, I was able to return to the country. Such was my dangerous but successful adventure.

* * * * * *

After arriving at the dock in Haiphong I boarded a train for Nghe An. By chance on the train I ran into an older province chief X[62] . . . of Thai Binh province. He was the type of person who is clever in flattering high officials. He wrote a few words on a small piece of paper and handed them to me. They read as follows:

"Before you had been gone a week, the police inspector had launched a massive search. You should make arrangements right away to escape. If you don't you will face danger."

I was quite worried. But I had not yet fulfilled the purpose for which I had returned to the country. There was no way I could flee now. I felt that I should go ahead and finish my work. Whatever was to happen would happen.

And so I fled back to Ha Tinh and arranged with my cohorts to sneak away to a meeting at the home of Dang Tu Kinh. After the meeting Dang brought the important papers to Hue to show them to Cuong De and then went immediately to Quang Nam and explained our plans to our comrades there and in Quang Ngai.

I wandered around the Nghe-Tinh area day after day, discussing our plans together with the members of the Association. Then I received a letter from my comrades in the capital and the immediate surrounding area urging me to waste no time in leaving the country. Since the Nghe-Tinh area was the area watched and spied upon most by the French, my comrades did not want me to postpone my departure from that dangerous spot any longer.

Fortunately I ran into Tran Dong Phong,[63] who gave me fifteen bars of silver[64] and 200 piasters to cover my travelling expenses and urged me to get on with my trip.

And so once again I took leave of my country.

   *   *   *   *   *   *

As I left I asked Dang Tu Kinh to stay in Hue to assist Dang Thai Than in escorting Cuong De abroad, to ensure that the escape was accomplished without a flaw. Then I wrote a letter reminding my compatriots that they must prepare and make ready a sum of money to buy and transport the weapons we needed for launching our uprising in the future.

At the beginning of the ninth month [of 1905] Nguyen Thuc Canh[65] and I set out from the Che-Giang ferry landing.

Towards the end of that month we reached Haiphong. We met a man whose name was Ly Tue and who worked as a houseboy on a French boat. He helped me work out a scheme to avoid danger.

Ly Tue was a brave man, a strategist and one who understood deeply the meaning of justice. Afterwards he was able secretly to help our Association a great deal. Helping me to find a way to get out of the country was the first time he had thrown himself into the affairs of the nation. He was truly one of zeal in the pursuit of justice. In the face of danger he knew no fear. As I set forth into fortune's buffeting winds I never expected to meet such a man. I understand that now he has been exiled. I am not sure whether he is dead or alive.[66]

* * * * * *

In the tenth month of that year I arrived in Yokohama and went to the boarding house I had stayed at before. There I saw a young Vietnamese student, Luong Lap Nham,[67] who had arrived before me. He appeared to be a man of enthusiastic character, disheveled in appearance. After sounding him out I learned that he had left Vietnam for Japan alone, arriving here with only three piasters in his pocket.

Seeing him I was both overjoyed and dumbfounded. He was a young fellow countryman who alone had dared to risk his life to brave the wind and waves to come to a faraway country that he had never seen or heard of before. Certainly Luong was the first one to do so. In fact it turned out that Luong had not yet spiritually prepared himself for such a venture. He had merely heard that I was in Tokyo and thus determined to abandon his home and country. How many young intelligent countrymen might there be after Luong?

At that time I was active in the area between Tokyo and Yokohama, usually joining together with some of the famous members of the Japanese Party with whom I had found mutual understanding. I relied on them a great deal to point out to me important points in the task that lay ahead.

As a result I realized again that the level of political understanding of our people was still terribly low and that we were lacking in individual skills and proficiency.[68] I was to regret that we had concentrated so much energy on the problem of weapons, without stopping to consider whether or not this was the best strategem to acquire our country's independence!

One day I came to the house of Liang Ch'i-ch'ao and during a brush-conversation I told him of my idea. He said to me:

"A strategy for the independence of your honorable country should have three main components. The first is the strength of your own countrymen in your own country. The second is aid from the two provinces, Kwangtung and Kwangsi. The third is Japanese aid.

"Kwangtung and Kwangsi can only help you with weapons. And Japan can only help you in the area of foreign relations. Ultimately, you must rely on the strength of your own country."

XII. I APPEAL TO THE YOUTH TO GO TO JAPAN TO STUDY

Liang Ch'i-ch'ao continued:
"The most important strength is that of individual knowledge and expertise [*nhan tai*]. And so I think the first strategem for your country should be to endeavor to cultivate that above all. As soon as you have acquired enough knowledge then you must just bide your time until an occasion arises when you might accomplish your task with ease."

I respected the words that Liang had spoken to me very much. I returned to my boarding house and, not being able to sleep, I lay awake thinking all night.

As I peered across the world it seemed like a flying dragon or a roaring tiger, like a flash of lightning and a torrent of clouds. There are a thousand different ways in which a man can be proficient, each of them different from one another. Even within this little corner of the world our country ranked the poorest a thousand times over. Why even try to compare us to Europe or America?

Thus our most urgent task was to nourish and develop our knowledge—we needed to talk about it no longer. But if we wanted to nourish our skills and abilities, how were we to go about it, for the real power of education rested in the hands of the French Protectorate government?

Yet in spite of all this there was no way that we could have reconciled ourselves to having our hands tied as we waited for death. There remained only one way, an appeal to the youth of Vietnam to wake up and risk their lives in coming abroad to study. In this way we would gain the freedom to develop our intellects and the country would quickly develop the skills it needed for the work that lay ahead.

I wrote a treatise appealing to our countrymen to contribute money for the young to come to Japan to study. It was a short treatise, only a few thousand words in length. Nevertheless, in a whole lifetime of writing it was this treatise that was to give me the greatest satisfaction.[69]

The reason for this was that the work I had done up till now had been in relation to the situation immediately before us. As for any durable long-term undertaking or strategy for the country, there was only this treatise. If it was to have any effect at all, our countrymen would go abroad to study more and more, our skills and abilities would develop increasingly and the level of political understanding of the people would grow higher. Surely Vietnam would be born again!

Yet before the study-abroad movement was five or six years old, the heavy and cruel oppression of the French was to make it the target of ten thousand different arrows, carefully aimed and fired. I had never foreseen this problem. Alas! My ability is so feeble, my strength so weak, there are a hundred tasks to do and not a single one accomplished. I am like the wandering soul of Tinh Ve,[70] who has run out of stones before the sea of anger has been filled. I float through night and day bobbing with the waves. How sorrowful!

Having finished writing *Khuyen Thanh Nien Du Hoc* (*Advice to Youth to Study Abroad*), I had a few thousand copies printed up and entrusted Tang Bat Ho to bring them back to Vietnam for distribution. In the twelfth month of the year of the Serpent [1905] Tang returned to Vietnam and campaigned eagerly among the students to come to Japan to study.

At the same time Nguyen Hai Than escaped from Vietnam to Japan and met with me in Yokohama. When he read my article he was overjoyed and offered to take on the responsibility of raising funds for propagandizing the idea of studying abroad among the students.

Not long afterwards news of my article spread and caused a controversy throughout the country.

In the first month of the Horse [1906] I went to the home of Inukai Tsuyoshi in order to discuss bringing over Vietnamese students and arranging for their schooling and a place for them to stay.

At that time Fukushima Yasumasa was head of the renowned Shimbu Military Academy in Tokyo. I asked him if three students, Nguyen Thuc Canh [pseudonym Tran Huu Long], Luong Lap Nham and Nguyen Dien might study at his school. Another student, Luong Nghi Khanh[71] was to study at the Asian Common Culture School [Dobun Shoin]. In all our four thousand year history there had never been a Vietnamese who had gone to study abroad until these four. Alas! With such a history, whoever says that our children are like old men bent with age is surely correct.

In the second month of that year [1906], Dang Tu Kinh and his group had escorted Cuong De to Hong Kong. He wrote to me in Japan and summoned me to Hong Kong. In all these years there was truly only this event to make us overjoyed and elated.

I was anxious to know about the situation in Vietnam as well as to have the opportunity to welcome Cuong De. And so at the end of the second month I took a boat from Japan to Hong Kong. There I met Phan Chau Trinh, who had just arrived from Vietnam.

Phan was making this trip because he was eager to observe the nature of Japanese civilization. After meeting me he joined me and Cuong De on a boat to Japan. We arrived in Yokohama towards the end of the fourth month.

I took Phan to see all the schools and famous places in Tokyo. I also had him meet many illustrious Japanese. A few weeks later he said to me:

"To look at the level of political understanding of the Japanese and compare it to our level of political understanding is no different from comparing a young chicken to an old hawk. No, sir, you are here; you should concentrate your energy on writing. You must awaken our people lest they remain deaf and blind. As for the task of leading development within the country, I shall try to take care of that. As long as I have my tongue, the French can't do anything to me that is worth worrying about."

I felt his words were very correct. I wrote the first volume of *Hai Ngoai Huyet Thu* [*Overseas Book Written in Blood*]. When

Phan Chau Trinh returned to Vietnam, I sent the book back with him.

According to my compatriots I was a man who stirred people, who rang the evening bell and beat the morning drum to wake people up. Surely this book was one that followed in the footsteps of *Ryukyu's Bitter Tears*.

Not long after, several members from the militant extremist faction in the Nghe-Tinh area, including Dai Dau and Than Son,[72] wrote to me—mostly to urge me on in the affair of obtaining weapons.

This problem alone caused me to waste I don't know how much energy and brought about deplorable, tragic failure—making me truly miserable!

While I admired the hot tempers of the militants, their minds were too fixed on recklessly pursuing one course of action—that of violence. Before I had gone abroad I had exactly the same idea. Not until I had left the country, broadened my knowledge and learned from foreigners did I understand that the task of restoring our country should have a truly stable foundation or else should not be attempted at all.

Thus, on the one hand, I was encouraging our youth to study abroad; while on the other hand, I wanted to develop the patriotism of all the people. I wrote *Tan Viet-Nam Ky Niem Luc* [*Anniversary of the New Vietnam*], *Viet-Nam Quoc Su Khao* [*A Study of Vietnam's National History*], and another volume of *Hai Ngoai Huyet Thu* [*Overseas Book Written in Blood*]. These books expressed with emotion and pathos the hope that our people would avoid the examples set by Champa[73] and Chenla.[74] Rather, the books continued, we should try to follow in the footsteps of the Trung Sisters[75] and the Kings of Le[76] in developing enthusiasm and taking our lives into our own hands while our race was not yet wiped out, our life not yet extinguished. If we did not, it would be too late.

XIII: I MEET HOANG HOA THAM

But I am truly stupid.

What if all our people were wise—then who could force us to

work as buffaloes and horses? What if our people knew how to love their country—then who could force us into slavery? Held firmly in the grip of the French as we are, if we were to raise our voices openly to speak out about patriotism or protecting our race it would be no different from sitting in front of some gangster and discussing ways of disposing of him. Surely anyone with some learning could have guessed quickly that my plans were sure to fail.

Nevertheless, in spite of the fact that I now had some such strategy, I still could not turn my face away in indifference to the request from those in the militant faction.

And so I decided that I must return to Vietnam for a second time. This time I had two purposes.

The first was to go to all strategically important points on the Kwangtung-Kwangsi/Vietnam border in order to inspect the terrain, make contact with the local leaders, and arrange for the transport of arms in the future.

The second was to go to Bac Giang and visit Hoang Hoa Tham to ask him to grant us a piece of land for use by those in the extremist faction. There they might wait until the day we resolved the weapons problem.

Alas! Weapons! Weapons! This was not a problem to be resolved in an instant. In truth, there wasn't a moment when I could feel that plans and preparations regarding weapons had gotten far, much less could they be looked back on as a mission accomplished.

In the seventh month of the year of the Horse [1906] I bid farewell to Japan and returned to Kwangtung. In Sa-ha I met Manh Hieu Cong[77] and the oldest child of Phan Dinh Phung, Phan Ba Ngoc,[78] who had just arrived from Vietnam.

Phan was younger than I but very bright and intelligent. In Vietnam I had a chance to talk deeply and intimately with him. Now that we ran into each other abroad I was overjoyed to meet such a close friend. I told him I wanted to return to Vietnam, and he declared his intention to go to Japan.

After taking leave of Phan, I hurried on to Kham-Chau, looking for a man from the old Can Vuong group by the name of Tien Duc.[79] I would rely on him as a guide. We went along the full length of the border from Tu-Chau, across Thai Binh district to Long-Chau and then crossed over the Nam Quan border pass. From beginning to end it took us altogether five weeks. All that dangerous terrain—I examined it all thoroughly. Tien Duc was a great help in this task.

Once through the Nam Quan pass I came to the market town of Van Uyen. In this town there was a military camp commanded by a French major. Whoever was without the proper pass granted by the French was not allowed through.

I was able to buy a pass from a Chinese businessman and was able to go through under the name Hoa Thuong. At that time there was no regulation requiring a picture of the bearer on the pass and thus I had no trouble. I took the train from Dong-Dang for Hanoi. At that time it was the beginning of the ninth month.

When the train arrived in Gia Lam station I got off and then set out on foot for Thai Nguyen. When I arrived at Cho Chu I went on to visit Liang San-ch'i [in Vietnamese, Luong Tam Ky].

As I passed through the district of Thai Binh I had a chance to meet the military commander, Tran The Hoa. I asked him to introduce me to Liang San-ch'i who was one of Tran's former followers.

Tran ordered one of his subordinates to take me to Liang's plantation. In Thai Nguyen, Liang was quite influential. He grew rice and raised buffaloes over nearly eight-tenths of the whole province. His followers were many and he was quite well supplied with weapons. The French government had appointed him Ambassador for Pacification in order to keep him in line.

When Tran's subordinate and I arrived Liang San-ch'i welcomed us very warmly. On this occasion I tried to talk him into turning against the Protectorate and aiding us in our resistance. Liang said:

"As soon as your army can defeat the Japanese army, then I will support you with the two provinces of Thai Nguyen and Bac Kan."

I discovered that he was the kind of man who will wait and see until something is almost accomplished by someone else before taking part himself. By himself he had no spirit of daring or of making progress. As our thunder had not yet echoed forth, he would not help us at all.

I stayed with Liang for a few days and then bid him farewell. I followed a mountain road through the forest to Bac Giang province and arrived at the military outpost of Phon Xuong, where I visited Hoang Hoa Tham.

Up to this time Hoang and I had established a relationship of mutual understanding, but only through correspondence. This was the first time we had met each other face to face.

At this time Dang Thai Than was in Hanoi and hearing that I was in Phon Xuong, came up to meet me. We asked Hoang to set aside a piece of land as an outpost where the Association members from Nghe-Tinh might gather. Hoang agreed immediately and took us around the area so that we might choose the place we preferred.

Meanwhile Dai Dau had also come up to the outpost. I reminded him of my suggestion that he and his comrades plan to farm this land while waiting for the proper opportunity for action.

Not long afterward the military outpost of "*Tu Nghe*" [Scholars of Nghe An] was established. This time at least my efforts produced some small result.

XIV. THE PROVISIONAL GOVERNMENT OF NEW VIETNAM

But then the French suddenly declared war on Hoang Hoa Tham, immediately rendering our arrangement for the land utterly impracticable. Alas! Weary but with courage I had set out on such a long journey only to bring about the failure of a dream. Is there anyone who has made so many plans only to meet unexpected misfortune? If that is not evidence of my feeble ability and my frail intelligence, then what is? Whoever follows my example in leading a rebellion in the future should learn from my mistakes and take a different path.

It was already the end of the tenth month [1906] when the arrangements for the land grant had been made. Secretly I went to Hanoi to meet Ngo Duc Ke[80] and all the Association members who had come up from Hue.[81] We talked over our task. Then I went up to Bac Ninh where I convened a secret meeting in the home of Noi Due.[82] Dang Thai Than and Le Vo came up from Nghe An to attend our meeting.

By this time news of my activities was spreading and a dragnet of French agents crept out like wolves and foxes in every direction in search of me. My comrades, fearing danger and misfortune, all advised me to leave the country immediately. And so once again I took leave of my people and went abroad.

By the middle of the twelfth month I had gone through the Nam Quan border pass. I followed the Kwangsi road to Ngo-Chau where I took the boat to Hong Kong. At the beginning of the second month of the year of the Goat [1907] I arrived in Hong Kong.

The essay I had written encouraging learning had become quite popular. Vietnamese youth were escaping the French and flocking abroad. From the center of the country came Nguyen Sieu and Lam Quang Trung. From the south came Dang Binh Thanh and Hoang Hung. From the north came Dang Tu Man, Dam Khanh,[83] etc.

They entered into this undertaking courageously, braving wind and rain, risking their lives in search of knowledge as they followed each other to Canton and Hong Kong. For this reason we set up an organization in Hong Kong to welcome the students and to collect money and prepare to oversee this work. I also set up the *Viet-Nam Thuong Doan Cong Hoi* [Vietnam Merchant Association] to help the work of the Association. This group was headed by Vo Man Kien.[84]

At that time those Vietnamese who had followed the French and come to Hong Kong to make a living also began to support our righteous cause.[85] They began to urge each other on with great enthusiasm to join our Association. Was this not a good indication that our national spirit had not completely died?

I only regret that I lack the ability to protect—that my strength is less than perfect. No sooner does the seed I sow begin to sprout up than the wind and rain blow it down and wash it away. No sooner had we given the Vietnam Merchant Association its name than before many years it was broken up by outside pressures. What a pity!

From the spring of the year of the Goat [1907] to the winter of the year of the Monkey [1908] was the period during which the greatest number of students went abroad to study. The responsibility I bore during that period was difficult and we were not well organized. I had to select those who would enter school. I had to take care of public relations. I had to raise money and build solidarity within our group—alone I had to shoulder all these responsibilities. All of a sudden it was as if I had become an envoy of Vietnam abroad as well as holding the office of Inspector-General. The well is deep but my arms short, the task is great but my skill feeble—I was incapable of continuing to bear my responsibilities.

At the same time we set up the *Tan Viet-Nam Cong Hien* [Vietnam Constitutionalist Association] as a kind of provisional government of Vietnam overseas.[86] Although this organization was a very modest one it had a very quick influence on the people's spirit at home.

Not long afterward in central and north Vietnam several French officers were suddenly assassinated, and the people urged each other not to pay taxes. As if they were out to catch tigers and panthers, the French then brought forth all their strength to struggle against our Association.

Alas! The French had ten thousand times more money and weapons than we. They were ten thousand times more clever and crafty than our people. And so how could our Association avoid failure?

About the time of the year of the Monkey [1908] or the year of the Rooster [1909] the French hired a group of clever and crafty foxes to spy on and arrest members of our Association. The number of spies in the country grew to double the number of students who had gone abroad to study.

Whatever secret policy or scheme we might use to bring money and information out of the country, the French government relied on their agents to learn everything down to the smallest detail as they sought ways to destroy and smash us completely.

The families and relatives of Association members grieved and even had to suffer imprisonment as the cruel and wicked

French agents let forth their arrogant howls across the country. If any of our members now wanted to escape from the country and go abroad, they could only crawl as naked earthworms—that was the only way.

It was the goal of French policy to block the transport of our supplies and cut off the route of our reinforcements. This was their one and only plan. At the same time, relying on an important clause of the Franco-Japanese Treaty,[87] they requested the Japanese government to arrest and turn over to them the leaders of our Association and to break up the group of Vietnamese students in Japan.

The students bore two great hardships—the end of their financial support and the cutting off of their contact with Vietnam. Thus caught in the wind of tragedy they were forced to leave Japan.

And not only that, the Japanese government confiscated all the books, notebooks and leaflets that I had had printed to campaign for our cause among the people. Cuong De and I were also deported by the Japanese government.

This failure was truly painful for me. I felt as if my skin had been peeled off, my flesh torn apart, and that no part of my body remained whole.

XV. WE WANT TO TRANSPORT WEAPONS BACK TO HELP HOANG HOA THAM

Alas! In the task of saving the country there is nothing more urgent than developing the skills and abilities of the people. And to develop the skills and abilities of the people there would be nothing more important than having a way to organize a group of students.

But having fallen into this situation, we did not have the ability or the strength to organize the students any more. Although we left the students with a determination and a will to persevere, they had to find a way to study by themselves.

And so at that time there were those like Chung Hao Sanh and Ho Hoc Lam[88] who went to Peking. Some, such as Nguyen

Tieu Dau[89] [Ba Trac], Nguyen Sien and Huynh Trong Mau, went to Kwangsi. Others, such as Ho Vinh Long and Dang Quoc Kieu,[90] went to Siam. There were also those such as Tran Trong Khac[91] and Hoang Dinh Tuan[92] who stayed in exile in Japan, posing as Chinese in order to study. And as the students drifted to new horizons they had to take care of themselves. As far as their spirit was concerned they were still a group of patriotic youths, but as to their formal status they were but a band of students helpless and adrift.

At that time what was I doing? Faced with the unfortunate situation of our dearly beloved students, I resigned myself to beating my breast and wailing in a flood of tears, hoping somehow to put an end to the problem. But, like a man seven meters tall, I had made a promise to my land that as long as I lived I would in no way evade my responsibility.

With a situation as bad as this there was no way I could keep myself from turning to the way of violence. I already knew that violence and suicide were acts committed by those of narrow learning with no ability to plan for the future. But if circumstances force us towards suicide, then I would prefer to die a violent death. For in violence perhaps there is one chance in a thousand that one might find success. In any case, as I thought it over I realized that if I were to give up violence at that time there would have been nothing more worth doing.

I want to know how Than Bao Tu sought military aid for the state of Sui. Yet where is the royal court of the Ch'in for us to stand and cry out for military reinforcements? I want to know how Viet Vuong Cau Tien resigned himself to avenge Ngo. But where is Coi Ke, where I might take shelter as I make preparations?[93] And I want to use literature to motivate the people and fulfill my duty to my country, but unfortunately there is no piece of soil where literature's message might be sown—what a tragedy! Not only that, our brothers and comrades in Vietnam sooner or later will be in danger of being arrested, imprisoned, deported or even of having their heads cut off. Alas! When any beast comes to the end of the road and there is no way out, he must struggle for his life or die.

In the fourth month of the year of the Rooster [1909], after much hardship and bitterness, the Association had raised a sum of money and sent it on to me. I entrusted it all to a Japanese store, relying on them to buy weapons for us.[94] Since we had chosen violence, in one way or another we had to get at least a few weapons.

Having bought the weapons I left Dang Tu Man in charge of bringing them secretly to Hong Kong. I was already in Hong Kong when the weapons arrived towards the end of the fifth month. Immediately afterward we heard the news from Vietnam that Hoang Hoa Tham was engaged in battle with the French and in serious difficulty. We felt that sending aid to Hoang would be a just and righteous act that should in no way be delayed. And so we sought a way to quickly transport the weapons back to Vietnam.

To transport weapons to central Vietnam surely we would have to go by way of Siam. Thus I set out at once for Bangkok, the capital of Siam, in search of a way to request the Siamese authorities to help us.

The Ministries in charge of the Army and Foreign Relations in Siam at that time were somewhat in favor of helping our revolutionary Association, but they were still discussing it with each other and were not yet able to reach a decision.

As I thought the problem over again I realized that the revolutionary party of China[95] was very experienced in the secret transportation of weapons. Thus I left Bangkok in haste for Singapore where I visited Chuong Binh Lan.[96] Chuong himself wrote a letter of introduction for me to one of the leaders of the Chinese revolutionary party so that I might arrange for help from them.

Having finished discussing this affair I went to a Chinese shipping company and negotiated with them the terms and cost of transportation. Barring any obstacle, the day and time of the shipment of our weapons had been fixed.[97]

I never suspected that our efforts in one direction would turn and go in the opposite direction. In the middle of the second month of the year of the Dog [1910] I returned from Singapore to hear the news that the Protectorate had launched a wicked assault on our Association. The leader of our group in Vietnam,

Ngu Hai [Dang Thai Than] had been killed. The work of the Association was laid bare and smashed. Many of our weapons were still concealed in Hong Kong due to a long delay. This news soon spread to the British authorities in Hong Kong. In all more than ten chests of weapons and ammunition were confiscated by the British government.[98] Found guilty of committing a crime, Canh Lam[99] was thrown in jail.

Damnation! The arrival of such cruel news was no different than the fatal stab of a knife into my plan for violent activity. On that occasion I recited a few lines of poetry that bring painful recollections:

> How many times have I worried for the country and my bitter tears fallen?
> The arrival of news from my homeland troubles my heart!
> There is no fire that can burn away all my sadness,
> And storm winds only fan my anger.

These verses describe clearly our plight at that time. Beginning in the third month of the year of the Dog [1910] I entered a terribly sad and lonely period.

Sometimes I had no news from Vietnam for many long months, and I could not keep up with anything there. The Protectorate government had a strict policy of examining my correspondence and confiscating money that was sent to us from Vietnam.

Sometimes someone working on a French boat passed through with a bit of news, but it was without exception heart-rending and frightening. If it wasn't news that Dam Ky Sanh[100] had been sent away, it was news that Le Vo had been arrested or that the severed head or dismembered body of this or that Association member had been put on display. Usually such news reached our ears via a signal from the ship's horn.

The French, wanting to show their authority by striking fear into those Association members hiding abroad, allowed only news that this or that Association member had been beheaded or killed to leak abroad.

Thus a day did not pass that I was not forced to live with such sickening and heart-breaking news.

I left for Canton, but the French military authorities bought off several Chinese detectives to make things difficult for me to the point that I no longer dared write to earn my living. Early in the evening I would go to the home of a fine old Chinese lady over seventy years old who, like Phieu Mau,[101] would feed me. Alas! She took care of me during a period of my life during which I was wandering, as dust blowing in the wind. I do not know how many times she fed me with never a thought to the future, never a hope of recompense. She treated me as would a Vietnamese mother. Even were she to cause me to die and bury me under the ground I would still be grateful to her. Her name was Chau Bach Linh.

XVI. CH'EN CH'I-MEI AND HU HAN-MIN HELP US

In the second month of the year of the Pig [1911] I returned to Siam. At that time a group of Association members including [Dang] Tu Kinh, [Ho] Vinh Long, Ngo Sanh [Dang Thuc Hoa][102] and Minh Chung were taking refuge in Siam. They encouraged each other to work hard, plowing and planting rice fields, raising chickens and ducks, while saving their energy for the days ahead. They wrote to me in Hong Kong urging me to join them.

I pondered the idea and, wanting to imitate Ngu Tu Tu[103] who bided his time in the old days by farming, took a boat for Siam.

When I arrived I went to live on the Ban Tham[104] farm and worked together with my brothers from dawn until dusk, in weather both foul and fair. We shared the bitterness and together found less sorrow in our idleness.

I led the life of a hard-working farmer for eight months. But during those eight months I felt a wonderful and unknown freedom. When I was thirsty there was a spring to drink from. When I was hungry I could pick fruit to eat. The painful recollection of all my pleasureless days was completely buried in a life of drinking in the morning dew and breathing in the fresh air. It was a pleasurable way of life for someone in a period of hardship. I could go nowhere else and thus I feel it is proper to relate this story.

At that time free and at leisure, I wrote many stories in *quoc ngu*,[105] such as the one about Le Thai To[106] or the one about

Trung Nu Vuong.[107] I wrote many songs that encouraged patriotism and a love for our people, a love for our race. I taught these songs to the people living on the farm till they knew them by heart. Sooner or later they would sing these songs to themselves just for fun. In this way I tried to sow seeds of revolution in this country of azure waters and green hills.

In the tenth month of the year of the Pig [1911] Phan Ba Ngoc came to Siam from Hong Kong with the news of the Wuhan uprising.[108] The news was deeply moving to me. Before, when I was in Japan, I had had the occasion to become acquainted with such Chinese revolutionary leaders as Hoang Khac Cuong and Chuong Thai Viem.[109] Together with Truong Ke[110] and other distinguished and well-educated gentlemen from Korea, Japan, India and the Philippines, we had organized the *Toa Domeikai* [East Asia United League, in Vietnamese *Dong A Dong Minh Hoi*]. We and they both came from that same class of people who had suffered the loss of their country and longed to restore their country's former estate. Our policies were by nature very compatible.

Now, hearing the news that the Chinese revolution had begun, I had the feeling that 'the gongs were clanging and the bells ringing their support for us.' On that occasion Phan Ba Ngoc advised me to return to China. Immediately I left the farm in Siam for China.

* * * * * *

Towards the end of the eleventh month I arrived in Hong Kong. Our comrades, who had been spread out in many places, also came together there at the same time.

At that time I wrote a political treatise entitled *Lien A Xo Ngon* [*Modest Proposal for an Asian Alliance*]. Its central point was an appeal to China and Japan to come together with one heart to change and improve the general situation in Asia.

As this treatise became known, it gained much praise and approval.

But the situation in Asia at that time had become entirely different from what we had anticipated. Thus we learned that the search for truth is not an easy task. We used to sit and engage in idle talk and wild ideas, making ourselves a laughing stock for others.

In the spring of the year of the Rat [1912] the Republic of China was established and the Chinese revolution completed. I went to Shanghai to seek out a trustworthy friend named Ch'en Ch'i-mei whom I had known in former days. Now he had become military commander of Shanghai. He gave me a large sum of money. For a long time I had been living in misery, with little money—no different from a man who had been starving for rice for a long time. Now, with this large sum of money that Ch'en Ch'i-mei gave me, I was overjoyed and relieved. Once again I had support for my activities.

While the Kuomintang in Kwangtung province was reveling in its success, the commander in chief, Hu Han-min, together with the police chief, Ch'en Chiung-minh, shared the feelings and ideas of our own revolutionary Association. I took this occasion to go to Canton where I intended to remain.

The Republic of China arose like a gust of wind that echoed and shook our country with great force. It gave great encouragement to the spirit of our people. Those of strong will encouraged each other to venture abroad, and a great many came to Canton.

Liet Sanh came with a small group from the south; [Nguyen] Hai Than and others came from the north; Dang Tu Kinh and Dang Hong Phan came with a group from Siam. They studied together in the same class at the Kwangsi Military Academy, while at the same time coming to Canton for meetings.

We had rented a house outside the city in order to form an association. Many came to live there, making it quite crowded.

Chinese socialist party members in Kwangtung such as Dang Canh A[111] and Liu Shi-fu also helped our Vietnam revolutionary group and campaigned on our behalf in all circles.

Since the Kwangtung authorities at that time were politely ignoring us, our organization was able to make some progress. We engaged in activities freely and securely, without any obstacle or worry. Profiting from this situation, our revolutionary group seemed quite encouraged.

My comrades advised and urged me to take advantage of this opportunity to launch the great undertaking.

52 Reflections from Captivity

Basically I am one who believes in militant activism, so the encouragement and approval from a majority of my comrades made me all the more determined to act. And thus the curtain was raised on the scene of our second tragic failure.

XVII. LUNG CHI-KUANG THROWS ME IN JAIL

On the fifth day of the fifth month in the year of the Rat [1912], those in the Association organized themselves as the *Hoi Viet-Nam Quang Phuc* [Society for the Restoration of Vietnam]. The comrades all asked that I remain as chairman. Hoang Trong Mau became the secretary.

We drafted a set of rules and regulations, set up the *Viet-Nam Quang Phuc Quan* [Army for the Restoration of Vietnam], and printed our own payment certificates for the army's internal use. In addition, we had innumerable books, articles and treatises printed that urged support for us, such as *Ha Thanh Liet Si [Martyrs of Hanoi]*[112] and an article of advice to the soldiers in the colonial army. We sent a man back to Vietnam with these books and ordered that they be distributed everywhere.

In the second month of the year of the Buffalo [1913] we appointed Nguyen Hai Than to be chairman of the *Hoi Viet-Nam Quang Phuc* along the Kwangsi province border with Vietnam. Tran Van Kiem became cell leader on the Siamese border. And in the direction of the Yunnan border Do Chon Thiet[113] volunteered to be in charge.

We agreed that whenever we began our task we would rise together on all three fronts. Thus we prepared and waited for the proper day and hour.

Nevertheless, at that time the group still had a difficult problem to resolve—that of finances. It was so difficult! We did not yet have sufficient money, and we worried over our lack of weapons and military supplies. Such misery! But if no unexpected calamity befell us, with time and good fortune we might be able to resolve this difficult problem. On the other hand, like a boat sailing against the wind that meets some unexpected catastrophe, our entire plan could break down and disintegrate like foam on the waves or fleeting clouds. Han Vo Han [also known as Gia Cat Khong Minh][114] lamented that in the course of one lifetime it is difficult to achieve satisfaction. How true!

In the summer of the year of the Buffalo [1913] there was an uprising in Canton against Governor Ch'en Chiung-minh. Ch'en fled and Lung Chi-kuang called in his troops and appointed himself governor of Kwangtung. At that time Lung and the revolutionary group of Vietnam did not know each other and had never shared any formal relationship. But Lung hated the followers of Hu Han-min and Ch'en Chiung-minh and sought only the opportunity to get rid of them. Our party thus was guilty by association. I was overcome with despair. Because of Hu and Ch'en our party could no longer consider Kwangtung a place of refuge.

At that point I wanted to leave quickly for somewhere else, but the work of the group was not yet completed. It would take a bit of time to put it all in order, so I resolved to stay on.

I also worried for my own safety. I wrote a quick letter to Nguyen Dinh Nam (i.e. Nguyen Thuong Hien),[115] relying on him to find a way to campaign on my behalf for a permit so that in the future I might be able to go somewhere else.

Nguyen was a man of great enthusiasm for our country. At the beginning of the seventh month he received my letter and was able to have the Ministry of Foreign Relations in Peking[116] send down a permit for me right away. With this permit in hand my worries were lessened.

At any rate there were quite a few of us in Kwangtung and if we all were to leave at the same time we would need some money. Since we had no money, we resigned ourselves to staying on together with no plans for going anywhere.

Not long after, we received news that the Governor-General of French Indochina was on his way to Kwangtung. The following week all our organizations were investigated and ordered to disband. I and an important leader of the group, Mai Lao Bang,[117] were thrown in jail. Before Hoang Trong Mau left for Yunnan, and as Phan Ba Ngoc set sail for Japan, they both warned me to avoid danger and find a way to escape from Kwangtung. But I realized that there were countless Association members in Kwangtung and that I should not allow myself to worry only for my own fate. And so as I hesitated, undecided, I became trapped by this terrible disaster. Such was the result of my stupidity and lack of courage.

When first arrested I felt that we would never come to the point of having to die. But when I saw how we were treated on the way to jail, sometimes handcuffed, sometimes tightly bound, and how we were thrown into a cell together with convicts condemned to death, I realized that Governor-General Lung Chi-kuang was not treating me as a political prisoner. I saw the hour of my death approaching!

From the time I went abroad until now, this is the first time I have tasted prison. Mai was ahead of me; this was his third time in jail.

After the first day in jail Mai and I were put together in the same cell. That night I consoled him by composing this poem:

> Helpless and isolated in a foreign land you and I,
> You alone have tasted enough bitterness.
> How many times you have come close to death!
> You have been thrown in jail three times already!
> Heaven has charged you with great responsibilities and so you
>   have made your resolutions.
> Surely in time the Lord will help you to succeed.
> If the road of life were entirely flat,
> How would we distinguish heroic and talented men from
>   anyone else?

And then I consoled myself with the following *nom*[118] poem:

> Still the patriot, still the gentleman on the move,
> With legs tired out, I come to rest in prison.
> At once the homeless guest of the four seas,
> And a wanted man on all five continents.
> I have taken firmly in hand the task of developing the land and
>   saving the people.
> I throw off my rancor with a laugh.
> As long as I live I shall pursue my mission.
> What use fear in the face of such dangers?

After composing these two poems I chanted them out loud and then burst out in a laugh that echoed around and beyond the four walls, as if I had forgotten we were locked up.

* * * * * *

After the second day Mai and I were placed in separate cells. From that day on I was but a jailbird, abandoned and alone on a piece of foreign soil.

In such deplorable and humiliating situations, when in jail, it is of course no use to lament one's pain. But there is the sorrowful fact that I have had to be separated from my brothers, without any news, with only myself to speak Vietnamese for myself to hear, thinking only of my sad destiny. I think of my failures and weep, my tears falling like torrents of rain. Truly, from the day I was born until now I have never known the taste of suffering as I know it now.

But I have arrived at this suffering because of the ambition that I have held for these last thirty years. And what has this ambition been?

It has been but a yearning to purchase my freedom even at the cost of spilling my blood, to exchange my fate of slavery for the right of self-determination.

Ah! With such an ambition I took in my own hands the supreme responsibility of speaking on behalf of my people. Is there anyone who dares say I should not have done this? Yet if such an ambition is to achieve anything great, we must rely on the toughness of our muscles, the excellence of our learning, the skill of our planning, and the careful manipulation of conditions. Instead, I wondered if at best I wasn't just a blind man leading the blind. Now I have failed simply because I am unskilled. I need complain no more.

However, I think that in this world there is no reason why a stream of water once it has flowed downward can never come up again, or why a life once set on its course cannot change. Who knows but that my failure today will not be good fortune for my people tomorrow?

Hark! The descendants of Hung Vuong[119] are not all yet dead, and the old story of Le Hoang[120] is repeated over and over. Let the thousands, ten thousands, even hundreds of thousands of my people who bear an ambition such as mine take heed from my failure. Let them become people who can take care of themselves. We must not wait until our finger has been cut the ninth time before we find the bandage.

I realize that I am a man who has not obtained steel weaponry worth holding on to, that on this earth I have laid down no strategy worth standing on. At most I am an empty-handed rogue with nothing to my name, weak in force and feeble in ability. Yet I am ready still to fight long-toothed tigers and sharp-clawed panthers. Those who understand my inner soul might console me by saying:

'What a brave man!'

Those who wish to look at my mistakes might well look down and say:

'What a stupid man!'

To sum up, in this world there is truly no one as stupid as I. If this be the last day of my life and if, upon my death, I still be called by such a forbidden name as 'the most stupid,' then this is very correct. It is impossible to call me anything else. But if I have the good fortune to survive and if, afterwards, I see tigers and panthers, then surely I will fight. May my people learn their lesson from my example.

> On the 25th day of the 12th month of the year of the Buffalo [1914] I Sao Nam write this *Nguc Trung Thu* in the Canton jail after the third day of my imprisonment.

Prison Diary

INTRODUCTION to Ho Chi Minh's *Prison Diary*

NGHE AN is a province poor in natural endowments yet rich in history. Ho Chi Minh was born there in 1890, twenty-three years after Phan Boi Chau. With an easy walk from either his paternal or his maternal village in Nghe An, Ho Chi Minh could climb a mountain from which with one sweep of the eye he could see the home regions of numerous illustrious ancestors. Before Ho was five or six we may assume he had listened to all the popular tales of resistance to Chinese, Mongols and French, not least of all because one of his maternal aunts was a well-known ballad singer of the region. Then, too, a maternal great-uncle was seized by the French and sent to Con Son prison island for having participated in a resistance organization. Three decades later this great-uncle would be released and live with Phan Boi Chau in Hue until the latter's death in 1940.

Ho Chi Minh's father, Nguyen Sinh Sac, had demonstrated scholarly potential from an early age.[1] It was not until 1894 that he scored high in the regional examinations and was able to go on seven years later to pass the metropolitan exams in the same class as the even more brilliant Phan Chu Trinh and Ngo Duc Ke. Unfortunately about the same time Ho Chi Minh's mother died of complications in childbirth. The family left the royal capital of Hue and returned to Nghe An, where Ho's father organized a systematic classical studies program for him. It was during these years that the young Ho sat in fascination at Phan Boi Chau's feet listening to him recite poetry. Yet, when Phan or one of his associates tried not long after to persuade the family to send Ho and his elder brother to Japan, it was decided that a program of French studies at the royal academy in Hue would be preferable.

This was a turning point for the 15-year-old boy. It focused his attention straight toward Europe instead of on Japan and China as cultural and political intermediaries, as was the fashion of Phan Boi Chau, Phan Chu Trinh and others of that generation. It brought him in direct contact with French colonial administrators, an experience that while hardly pleasant was at least instructive. Perhaps most importantly, it caused Ho Chi Minh to be present in Hue in April 1908 when thousands of angry, impoverished peasants marched into the town to protest at colonial taxes and forced labor and were attacked brutally by French infantry. As a result of such violent altercations throughout central Vietnam in 1908, the French imprisoned scores of scholar-gentry leaders, leaving young men like Ho Chi Minh with some stark questions about what they should be doing with their lives. Soon Ho's own father, by now a district magistrate in Binh Dinh province, had incurred the displeasure of the French *Résident* and was removed. Rather than return to Nghe An, Ho's father traveled south to Saigon. Ho abruptly halted his studies in Hue and by late 1911 was also in Saigon, now determined to find a way to get to Europe.

With an ingenuity that would characterize his entire career, Ho Chi Minh signed on as a galley assistant on a French merchant ship. He spent two or more years working from one port to another, then settled in London during the early years of World War I and took an intense interest in the Irish uprising. Toward the end of 1917 he crossed the channel to Paris and came in close contact with Phan Chu Trinh, both of them subsisting by using their calligraphic brushes to retouch photographs. Soon Ho was circulating within French trade union, leftist intellectual and pacifist circles. He developed enough confidence in his own ideas and his command of the French language to begin publishing articles in leftist newspapers and journals.

In December 1920 Ho Chi Minh attended the French Socialist Congress at Tours as 'the delegate from Indochina.' He jousted sharply with moderates over their failure to pay enough attention to the colonial question, to imperialist oppression and exploitation in distant lands. It was on this basis, in fact, that he joined the rump French Communist Party and was subsequently appointed to attend a major Comintern meeting in Moscow. As a member of the new standing committee on colonies Ho was then on his way to China with Mikhail Borodin. There he quickly contacted Phan Boi Chau and other Vietnamese émigrés and, along with Liang Chung-k'ai, set about organizing the League of East Asian Oppressed Peoples.

By early 1925 Canton was something of an anti-imperialist Mecca, and the Vietnamese were probably the largest foreign group represented. Most were in their twenties or even younger. Although educated in the new Franco-Vietnamese colonial schools, they were clearly dissatisfied with what they had seen and been taught. Otherwise they would never have risked illegal exit and a life of constant pursuit by the highly efficient French *Sûreté*. More receptive to twentieth century intellectual currents than the preceding generation of Confucian-educated scholar-gentry, they tended to regard Phan Boi Chau with the quiet respect one would give a battered old warrior rather than as a source of fresh ideas or political initiatives. By contrast, Ho Chi Minh, being older than most of the arriving activists but much younger than Phan Boi Chau, had both knowledge of traditional thought and first-hand experience with modern institutions, political organizing and ideology. Through the Comintern and other associations Ho had already fashioned an invaluable network of relations with other groups and individuals in China, the Soviet Union, France, Germany, England and Thailand, all of them also dedicated to the smashing of imperialism.

Ho Chi Minh appears to have requested and obtained Phan Boi Chau's support for the Comintern-sponsored League of East Asian Oppressed Peoples. Unfortunately while Phan was away from Canton several Vietnamese émigrés apparently plotted with the French *Sûreté* to capture him. As mentioned in the introduction to Phan Boi Chau's *Nguc Trung Thu* this was accomplished in Shanghai, and Phan was transported to Hanoi, brought before the colonial Criminal Commission in November 1925 and sentenced to life imprisonment. Subsequently he was taken to Hue, where he lived out the remaining 15 years of his life in guarded "retirement." Some eight years after Phan Boi Chau's death anti-communist Vietnamese circulated the story that Ho Chi Minh, then President of the Democratic Republic of Vietnam, was somehow implicated in Phan Boi Chau's 1925 capture. Suffice it to say that no one ever advanced solid evidence for this assertion, least of all the French *Sûreté*, which presumably would have been delighted to try to discredit the patriotic credentials of Ho Chi Minh.[2]

By 1930 Ho Chi Minh and his comrades, now numbering several thousand in and out of Vietnam, felt competent enough to request and receive recognition from the Comintern as a full-fledged Marxist-Leninist organization, the Indochinese Communist Party (Dang Cong San Dong Duong). However, operations suffered a grave setback one year later after the French smashed the peasant "Soviets" in Nghe An and Ha Tinh provinces and then proceeded to capture most of the Party Central Committee, not to mention many liaison cadres. Ho Chi Minh himself was arrested by British police in Hong Kong and was quite lucky only to be ejected from the colony rather than being turned over to the French. There followed the slow regeneration of Party organization, now drawing heavily for leadership on several score Vietnamese who had benefited from up to three years intensive revolutionary training in Moscow. During the Popular Front period (1935-38) there was a substantial increase in Party membership and mass influence. But once again, after the sweeping French crackdown of 1939-40 the Party had to begin reconstructing almost from scratch. It was becoming both the Party's bitter woe, in terms of friends dead or imprisoned, and its special capability, since no other Vietnamese anticolonial organization showed itself nearly as competent in surviving and rebuilding.

In 1940, having undertaken diverse Comintern responsibilities for almost a decade, Ho Chi Minh was able finally to return to South China and to resume direct leadership of the Indochinese Communist Party. Crossing the border into Vietnam, he guided the Party Central Committee towards forming, in May 1941, the League for the Independence of Vietnam (Viet-Nam Doc Lap Dong Minh Hoi), popularly known as the Viet Minh. National liberation was given strategic priority over social revolution. Formation of armed proselytizing teams in mountainous and rural areas was stressed over clandestine organizing in the cities. The Viet Minh was also to be the most important group to openly declare affiliation with the Allied struggle against the Axis, a position that in Vietnam in 1941 seemed faintly ridiculous but by early 1945 was shown to be farsighted and a potent asset in mobilizing tens of thousands of supporters against lingering Japanese-Vichy French rule.

In an effort to improve contacts with those same Allies, Ho Chi Minh in August 1942 set out from the mountains of northern Vietnam for the Kuomintang wartime capital of Chungking, more than 500 miles distant. However he had hardly crossed the border into China when he was arrested by local Kuomintang police. They do not appear to have known who he was. The fact that he was a foreigner travelling without authorization papers was reason enough in wartime China for detention, or worse. Besides, the simple clothes, the unassuming manner of this man never quite concealed the presence, the unshakable sense of purpose that always impressed observers. Clearly he was not just another idle wanderer.

So while they waited for higher instructions the police put Ho Chi Minh in shackles along with the petty gamblers, diseased prostitutes, opium addicts and family members of deserting soldiers. For 14 months Ho was shuttled through all thirteen districts of Kwangsi province and incarcerated in a total of thirty different jails. Conditions were terrible, as Ho's poetry makes us see. For many months he seems to have been able to endure by applying a dose of ironic humor to whatever new misfortune befell him. And there were always the sights or sounds of nature to divert him, realities that the guards could never change for the worse. In later months, nevertheless, Ho's poetry took on an almost desperate quality and one must wonder how much longer he could have retained his sanity.

Fortunately about this time Ho Chi Minh was transferred to the Liuchou military prison, identified as a "political prisoner" of some status, given enough food to eat, allowed to sit in his cell unshackled and even to read an occasional book or newspaper.[3] The Kuomintang authorities now knew he was a member of the Viet Minh leadership. They almost certainly recognized him as the same individual who had founded the Indochinese Communist Party and who had associated intimately with their bitter enemies, the leaders of the Chinese Communist Party.

What to do with him was another question. It was silly to be nice to a group of Vietnamese Marxist-Leninists, especially since the Kuomintang also had with them several non-communist organizations of Vietnamese émigrés, for use as the situation required. On the other hand, Kuomintang and American intelligence experts were always pressing for more information on Japanese activities in Indochina. The U.S. Army Air Force needed contacts in the mountains of northern Vietnam to assist downed pilots. By late 1943 they were looking increasingly to the Viet Minh for such assistance.

Something of a compromise was struck, whereby Ho Chi Minh was released from prison in the fall of 1943 and allowed to exercise his wobbly legs in the hills of South China but prevented from returning to Vietnam. Members of the non-communist émigré groups complained to the Kuomintang about the increasing influence of the Viet Minh and backed out of an arrangement whereby several of them were to go back to Vietnam with Ho Chi Minh. Finally General Chang Fa-kwei, the Kuomintang area commander, permitted Ho to make his way back alone. Almost two years after departing Ho rejoined his delighted comrades. He would not be jailed again.

Ho Chi Minh's *Nguc Trung Nhat Ky* (*Prison Diary*) is in the first instance a sparse record of this painful odyssey.[4] Whenever he felt like crying out, whenever he had a new thought or creative image that seemed worthy of remembering, Ho would unfold his few scraps of paper and scribble a poem or two. More often than not he employed the T'ang dynasty seven-syllable-to-a-line quatrain. It was a poetic medium well known to Vietnamese versed in classical Chinese. Besides, to have written in Vietnamese *nom* (demotic script) or *quoc ngu* (romanized script) would have been quite dangerous since the prison authorities could not have read it, and they would immediately have suspected him of secret, subversive communications. For the same reason Ho mostly avoided overt political statements in his prison poetry. He felt no restraint in criticizing his captors for forcing a fellow ally to rot away uselessly. And the gross injustices suffered by other prisoners were worthy of

Ho's sharp comment, too. The reader will search in vain, however, for affirmations of class struggle, annihilation of the oppressor or belief in dialectical materialism. In one quatrain he does make hidden reference to the flag of the Viet Minh, and in another famous poem he speaks of the "true dragon" flying out to action once the cage is unlocked. But that is mild fare indeed for a man who lived in order to organize the Vietnamese revolution.

Perhaps we have stumbled here upon one of the reasons why Ho Chi Minh's *Prison Diary* is likely to be read and remembered long after most of his speeches to Party congresses or his public exhortations to the Vietnamese people at large. Ho Chi Minh in jail, perpetually harassed by lice, leg irons, scabies, hunger, cold and lassitude, distressed at possessing only scant amounts of paper to write on and wanting to avoid polemics that would anger his captors, was forced to reduce things to their most fundamental aspects. Life was precious, he pointed out, in so many small but significant ways. Liberty was even more important, so that that *Prison Diary* can also be read as a poignant metaphor on the fettering of all Vietnamese under French colonial rule. And happiness was as much a state of mind, a healthy way of looking at the world, at people, at oneself, as it was a set of objective physical conditions or material benefits.[5]

One of Ho Chi Minh's most revealing thoughts is contained in the little quatrain titled "Midnight":

> All faces have a harmless look in sleep.
> Awake, men differ: good and evil show.
> No virtue and no vice exists at birth—
> of good and evil nurture sows the seeds.

It seems to me a profoundly human statement. There is the belief in the perfectibility of man, shared by both Confucianism and Marxism; not a shred of original sin here.[6] Yet it is not a simple paean to optimism; vice and evil get as much attention as virtue and good. Awake, men can be led to criminal acts just as easily as heroic behavior. The secret is in the creation of a fertile environment, which Ho Chi Minh always worked at more by means of personal example than by elaborate exegesis. And he was willing to forgive those who erred, providing they made an honest break with their past.

In a few years all of Ho Chi Minh's contemporaries and immediate disciples will be dead. It will be fascinating to observe whether his message of simplicity, directness, forgiveness and humor is capable of being transmitted to the younger generation. For the first time in 117 years Vietnam is free of foreign intervention. There is a whole new life to be built, an unprecedented opportunity to nurture good and divert evil. How it all works out will be an instructive lesson, not only for Vietnam but for the world.

D.G.M.

PRISON DIARY
by Ho Chi Minh

Prison Diary

The body stays in jail.
The mind goes free outside.
To reach the highest goal,
the mind must leap and soar.

Beginning the Diary

I've never cared for humming verse.
But what to do inside a jail?
I'll hum some verse to pass long days.
I'll hum and wait till freedom comes.

Arrested on Perfect Glory Street

On Perfect Glory Street I met with shame.
They meant to thwart my path and slow me down.
Out of thin air they spun a spying charge
and threw away the honor of a man.

Entering Chingsi District Prison

Old inmates take the freshman in.
Above, white clouds pursue black clouds.
White and black clouds have flown away.
One stays in jail who should go free.

Rough is the Road of Life

I

I safely climbed the steepest heights,
yet fell a cropper on the plains.
The tigers spared me in the hills—
men on the plains took me to jail.

II

On behalf of the Vietnamese,
I came to visit leaders in China.
But on my way a storm broke loose—
the guest was ushered into jail.

III

An upright man with conscience clear,
I'm called a traitor to the Chinese.
The world, no easy place before,
is getting all the tougher now.

Morning

I

Each dawn, rising over the wall,
the sun shines on the bolted gate.
The prison's still immersed in gloom,
but daylight's surging far ahead.

II

On waking up, all hunt for lice.
Eight o'clock gong—it's breakfast time.
My friend, eat well and get your fill.
At lowest ebb, your luck will turn.

Noon

The midday nap is such a balm!
Deep slumber lasts for hours and hours.
I mount a dragon, go to heaven . . .
Then I wake up—back in my cell.

Afternoon

At two, they open the air hole.
We all look up to glimpse the sky.
On high, free spirits, do you know
one of your kind is kept in thrall?

Evening

Past dinner, westward sinks the sun.
Folk tunes and ditties all burst forth.
This Chingsi jail, despite its gloom,
sounds rather like a music school.

PRISON FOOD

At mealtime, just one bowl of reddish rice.
No salt, no greens—no broth to wash it down.
If someone brings you food, you eat your fill.
If not so lucky, cry for Mom and starve.

A FELLOW PRISONER PLAYS THE FLUTE

Inside the jail I hear a homesick tune.
It sings of hope forlorn, it sings of grief.
Beyond all streams and passes, sorrow-struck,
a woman climbs upstairs to gaze afar.

LEG IRONS

I

Like monsters with their hungry mouths,
they swallow human legs at night.
They clench the right leg in their jaws,
leaving the left to bend and stretch.

II

Strange things do happen in this world!
Men fight to have their legs locked up.
Once shackled, they can sleep in peace.
Till then, no place to lay their heads.

LEARNING TO PLAY CHESS

I

To kill the time, let's take up chess.
Soldiers and horsemen, all give chase!
Move back and forth with lightning speed.
High skill and nimble feet shall win.

II

Look far ahead and plan with care.
Attack, and then attack some more.
Two chariots save not a wrong move.*
One pawn in time will turn the tide.

III

Two forces balance at the start.
The prize will go to but one side.
Perfect both offense and defense—
you'll earn the title of war chief.

* In Chinese chess, the two "chariots" are the most powerful pieces for each side.

WATCHING THE MOON

In prison there's no alcohol nor flower.
With what to celebrate this lovely night?
I go to the window and watch the moon.
The moon peers through the window at the poet.

WATER DOLE

Just half a basin for each man.
Wash up? Brew tea? Please suit yourself.
If you wash up, forget the tea.
If you want tea, then don't wash up.

MID-AUTUMN FESTIVAL

I

Mid-autumn moon—a mirror full and round.
It beams its silvery splendor on the world.
You all who wine and dine in your own homes,
forget not those who feast on grief in jails.

II

Prisoners celebrate mid-autumn too.
Their autumn moon and wind are tinged with gloom.
I can't gain freedom and enjoy the moon—
my heart follows its trail to roam and roam.

GAMBLING

You gamble, they arrest you—it's the law.
Once jailed, you're free to gamble in broad day.
Those gamblers, caught and jailed, can now lament:
"I should have known and come here from the first!"

Jailed Gamblers

The state won't feed those gamblers jailed—
let them repent their sinful ways.
Those who can pay dine on rich fare.
The poor just drool and swallow tears.

Transferred to Tienpao on "Double Ten" Day*

All homes are decked with lanterns and with flowers.
A people celebrates its day of joy.
This day, I'm hustled to another jail.
Contrary winds will thwart an eagle's flight.

   * Observance on the tenth of October (10-10) commemorated that day in 1911 when Chinese army units near Hankow rebelled against the Manchu government.

On the Road

He knows the road is rough who walks the road.
One mountain range, another mountain range . . .
Keep struggling up and reach the highest peak:
ten thousand miles will come within your ken.

Nightfall

Tired birds are flying, homebound, to the woods.
A lonely cloud is sailing through the sky.
Some mountain girl is busy grinding corn.
The corn once ground, the oven will glow red.

Overnight Stop in Lungch'an

My own "two horses" trot and trot all day.
I feast on "five-spice chicken" every night.*
Cold drafts and bedbugs are attacking me.
I'll gladly hear an oriole hail dawn.

    * At night a prisoner is bound hand and foot the way a fowl is trussed up for the dish called "five-spice chicken".

T'ientung

A bowl of thin rice gruel—that's a meal.
The hungry stomach groans and groans for more.
It doesn't fill you up, three yüan of rice,
when grains of rice cost as much as rare pearls.

Arrival at T'ienpao Prison

I walked fifty-three kilometers today.
Hat and clothes soaking wet, shoes torn to shreds.
No place to call my bed the livelong night—
I'll wait for daybreak, perched on the latrine.

Visiting her Husband in Prison

He is inside the iron bars.
His wife is outside, looking in.
Within mere inches of each other,
they're worlds apart like sky and sea.
What need be said that mouths can't say,
their eyes try somehow to express.

Before each word their tears well up—
a sight that pains and grieves the heart.

News Report: Willkie Given a Warm Reception*

Both you and I are China's friends.
We both are heading for Chungking.
You're sitting in the seat of honor—
meanwhile I'm lying low in jail.
Both you and I speak for our countries—
why don't they treat us the same way?
Coldness towards one, warmth towards another—
so goes the world as streams flow to sea.

  * In 1942, as President Franklin D. Roosevelt's unofficial envoy, Wendell L. Willkie was going to Chungking, headquarters of Chiang Kai-shek's Kuomintang government during World War II.

A Word to Myself

Without the cold and gloom of winter,
there'd be no warmth and light in spring.
Hard times have forged and tempered you,
turning your spirit into steel.

Country Scene

When I first came, the rice was green.
Now half the harvest's been brought in.
All peasants' faces smile and laugh.
The rice fields come to life with songs.

Gruel Stall

By the roadside, under a tree,
there's a thatched hut they call an "inn."
It serves cold gruel with white salt.
Still it's a place to stop and rest.

Kuoteh Prison

This prison is your home, sweet home.
Rice, wood, oil, salt—all must be bought.
A stove in front of every cell:
all day, soup simmers and rice boils.

Departure before Dawn

I

The cock's crowed once—the night's not yet dispersed.
A suite of stars escorts the moon uphill.
The traveler's setting out on his long road.
Raw gusts of autumn wind lash at his face.

II

The pallor in the east has now turned red.
All shreds of darkness have been swept away.
A flood of warmth engulfs the universe.
Inside the wayfarer the poet stirs.

From Lungan to T'ungcheng

Plenty of land, but barren soil.
That makes the folk work hard and save.
A spell of drought in spring, they say.
They've reaped three tenths of the hoped-for crop.

On the Way

Both arms and legs are tightly bound.
Birdsongs and flower scents fill the hills.
No one forbids me such delights.
I feel less lonely on the long road.

T'ungcheng (November 2)

T'ungcheng can rival Pingma jail.
A bowl of gruel still fills not.
Plenty of light and water, though.
And twice a day they air the cell.

A Jailmate's Paper Quilt

A patchwork of old books and new:
better a paper quilt than none.
Asleep on silk and jade, do you know
that many eyes can't close in jails?

Cold Night

Cold autumn night—no mattress and no quilt.
Hunch the back, fold the legs—you still can't sleep.
Bleak moonlight on the plantains adds its chill.
Look through the bars—the Dipper has lain down.

Fetters

A dragon coils about my arms and legs.
An officer with epaulets—that's me!
Those foreign fringes are made of gold braid.
But my own fringes are a rope of hemp.

Good-by to a Tooth

You're made of hard and sturdy stuff,
unlike that soft, long-stretching tongue.
We've shared the bitter and the sweet.
Now you go east and I go west.

The Wife of a Deserter

One day you went away for good.
You left me home to nurse my grief.
The state, deploring my sad plight,
asked me to come and live in jail.

In Jest

The state supplies free bed and board.
The guards on shifts provide escort.
I tour the country, seeing sights.
That's the grand way a man should live!

On the Way to Nanning

Hard irons have replaced the rope of hemp.
They tinkle like jade bracelets at each step.
I got locked up in prison as a spy.
But like some erstwhile potentate I strut.

Guards Carry Pigs

I

Guards carry pigs along the way.
Pigs get a lift—I'm pushed and shoved.
A man is treated worse than pigs
when of his freedom he's been robbed.

II

Of all the bitter woes on earth,
the loss of freedom hurts the most.
They watch your every word and deed.
They drive you like a horse or cow.

A Stumble

It was pitch-dark—still we had to set out.
The road was bumpy, hard to walk upon.
I stumbled and was thrown into a pit.
I managed to get out, but might not have.

On a Boat to Nanning

The boat floats down the river toward Nanning.
With legs strung up, I'm like a gallows bird.
Many a bustling hamlet on both banks.
And in midstream a swarm of fishing boats.

Nanning Prison

A "modern" building is this jail.
Electric lights are on all night.
Each meal is still a bowl of gruel.
The stomach grumbles and protests.

A Fit of Despondency

War's raging—the blue skies are set ablaze.
All soldiers race to battlefronts and fight.
Inaction weighs more heavily in jail.
A manly will won't fetch a pennyworth.

Listening to the Cock's Crow

You're just a common, ordinary cock.
Dawn after dawn you crow and herald day.
One cry arouses people from their dreams.
Yours is no common, ordinary job.

A Jailed Gambler Dies

His body was all skin and bones.
Pain, hunger, cold—too much to bear.
Last night, he still slept by my side.
Now he's left for the nether world.

Yet One More

Po and Shu would not eat the corn of Chou.*
The jailed gambler would feed on no state gruel.
Po and Shu starved to death on Mount Shouyang.
The gambler starved to death in a state jail.

  * According to Chinese tradition, Po I and Shu Ch'i were two princely brothers who, out of loyalty to their lord, would rather starve to death on Mount Shouyang than "eat the corn of Chou" whose ruler they condemned as a usurper.

No Smoking

No smoking—it's forbidden here.
Your tobacco lands in *his* pouch.
He'll put it in his pipe and smoke.
Just try a puff—he'll handcuff you.

Sundown

The wind—a sword's edge honed on rocks.
The cold—a spearhead piercing trees.
A distant bell quickens our steps.
Flute-playing boys drive buffaloes home.

Price Scale

To get rice cooked costs sixty cents.
Hot water sells for a whole yüan.
One yüan gives you sixty cents' worth.
That's how the prices go in jail.

A Sleepless Night

The first night-watch is gone—the second, the third . . .
I toss and turn—I fidget, get no sleep.
Fourth watch, fifth watch . . . As soon as my eyes close,
I see the star with five points in my dream.*

* The Viet Minh banner, eventually adopted as the official flag of the Democratic Republic of Vietnam, consisted of a five-pointed gold star on a red background.

Thinking of a Friend

That day, I told you by the river's edge:
"I shall return when the new crop is ripe."
Now the rice fields must have been plowed again.
I'm still a captive in a foreign land.

Writing a Petition for a Jailmate

We are in the same boat—could I say no?
On your behalf I wrote to those above.
I learned to say "whereas," "pursuant to" . . .
How much you thanked me for my little help!

Scabies

Our bodies wear brocade in red and blue.
We play upon the lute, plucking all day.
Brocade becomes us, honored guests of state.
Fellow musicians, we all pluck the lute.

Listening to the Pounding of Rice

Under the pestle groans the grain.
Yet pounding makes it cotton-white.
It's much the same with a man's life—
misfortune hones him into jade.

The Eleventh of November

I

Before, on each eleventh of November,
the end of Europe's conflict was observed.
Today, five continents are steeped in blood—
a war the wicked Nazis have provoked.

II

China has fought for almost six years now.
Her gallantry is known throughout the world.
Though victory has come within her grasp,
she must strive harder and counterattack.

III

Against Japan all Asian flags unfurl.
They come in various sizes, large and small.
The larger flags are needed for the fight.
But can the little ones be done without?

AIR RAID WARNING (November 12)

Enemy planes come shrieking in the sky.
The place is emptied as all flee and hide.
To dodge the warplanes we're let out of jail.
When one's let out of jail, it's cause for cheers.

WORDPLAY

A man, once freed from jail, will build his country.
Misfortune is the test of loyalty.
He earns great merit who feels great concern.
Unlock the cage—the true dragon will fly.*

---

* The poem can be read as translated, or it can be literally interpreted as an elaborate play on some Chinese characters and their components:

    Replace 人 (*jen* "man") by 或 (*huo* "probability") in 囚 (*ch'iu* "prisoner") and you get 國 (*kuo* "country, nation").

    Remove the head-particle from 患 (*huan* "misfortune") and you get 忠 (*chung* "loyalty").

    Add 人 (*jen* "man") to 憂 (*yu* "worry, concern") and you get 優 (*yu* "merit").

Remove 竹 (*chu* "bamboo") from 籠 (*lung* "cage, jail") and you get 龍 (*lung* "dragon").

The last line is especially significant if we recall that Ho Chi Minh once wrote a satirical skit in which King Khai Dinh, who collaborated with the French, was sarcastically dubbed a "bamboo dragon."

"Boardinghouse"

New "boarders" must, so goes the rule,
lie down at night near the latrine.
If they desire a good night's sleep,
let them come up with some hard cash.

Morning Sun

The morning sun shines through the jail.
It burns all mist and gloom away.
The breath of life pervades the world.
Prisoners' faces beam with smiles.

Unrest in Vietnam (News reports in the Nanning press)

Oh, sooner death than the life of a slave!
The banners of revolt are flying high.
Locked up in jail, grieving a captive's lot,
I wait to rush onto the battlefield.

A British Delegation in China

Americans had left, then Britons came.
They're lionized and feted everywhere.
I was sent over, too, as China's friend.
A special kind of welcome I've received!

Transferred Back to Wuming

They dragged me off to Nanning.
Now I'm dragged back to Wuming.
Shifting me to and fro,
they stretch and stretch my road.
It's outrageous!

Dogmeat in Paohsiang

They eat fresh-caught fish in Kuoteh.
They feast on dogmeat in Paohsiang.
These prison wardens, after all,
know on occasion how to live.

Road Menders

Lashed by wind, drenched with rain, you get no rest.
A toilsome, wretched life road menders live.
Of those who daily travel back and forth,
how many ever thank you for your work?

To My Walking Stick, Stolen by a Guard

A lifetime of uprightness and strength.
Through fog and snow we journeyed hand in hand.
Cursed be the knave who parted you from me!
He caused two friends an everlasting grief.

A Milestone

Neither high up nor far away,
neither an emperor nor a king,
you're just a little slab of stone,
set upright on the highway's edge.
Yet your instructions men will heed
so they won't stray from the right path.
You counsel them which road to take,
the longer route or the short cut.
You render them no little help.
They will remember what you do.

The Child in Pinyang Prison

Wa! Wa! Waa! Daddy ran away,
too scared to fight and save the country.
So, barely half a year of age,
I followed Mommy into jail.

Lighting Fee

On entrance pay a lighting fee.
Everyone must disburse six yüan.
Inside the prison realm of shades,
six yüan is all that light is worth.

Prison Life

Each prisoner has his own stove,
a full array of pots and pans.
He cooks the rice, boils greens, brews tea . . .
No end of fire and smoke all day.

Mr. Kuo

Duckweed and water met—we briefly talked.
He treated me with kindness, Mr. Kuo.
"A bit of coal in winter"—no great gift.
But it does prove such people still exist.

Mr. Mo, Head Warden

Generous Mr. Mo, Pinyang head warden.
To feed his prisoners, he pays for rice.
At night he lets them sleep in peace, untied.
He uses kindness, never wields brute force.

On the Train to Laipin

For weeks I toiled my way on foot.
Today I get to go by train.
My seat is just a heap of coal—
compared with legwork, it's first class.

A Man Attempts to Escape

To flee for freedom—his one thought.
He risked his life, jumped off the train.
He ran for half a mile, in vain.
They captured him and brought him back.

Laipin

The warden gambles every day.
The police captain shakes you down.
The prefect putters by his lamp.
It's peace as usual in Laipin.

Arrival in Liuchow

All horrors on this earth must sometimes end.
Today, the ninth, I arrive in Liuchow.
A nightmare of over a hundred days—
I've now waked up, but it still haunts my face.

Long Detention Without Interrogation

A bitter cup tastes bitterest at the dregs.
A rough roadway feels roughest toward the end.
The prefect's office is a mile away—
why am I kept waiting forever here?

Midnight

All faces have a harmless look in sleep.
Awake, men differ: good and evil show.
No virtue and no vice exists at birth—
of good and evil nurture sows the seeds.

At the Prefect's Office

A final pass to cross, I thought.
My day of freedom would soon dawn.
Alas, there's yet another pass—
I'll be transferred now to Kweilin.

After Four Months

"One day in jail—a thousand years outside."
The ancient saying's not far from the truth.
Four months of life unfit for humankind
have worn and aged me more than ten full years.

Indeed

For four months I've not had enough to eat.
For four months I've not slept a good night's sleep.
For four months I've not got a change of clothes,
and for four months I've taken not one bath.

And so

One of my teeth has fallen off.
My hair has turned to silver gray.
Gaunt and dark as a famished ghost,
my body's full of mange and sores.

Fortunately

I've borne up and endured.
I've yielded not one inch.
The body's racked with pain.
The spirit stays unbowed.

Seriously Ill

China's erratic weather hurts my health.
My heart so aches for my homeland, Vietnam.
To stay in prison and fall ill—o woe!
I should be crying but I'll madly sing.

Arrival in Kweilin

No "cinnamon" nor "forest" in Kweilin.*
You only see high mountains and deep streams.
The jail looms spectral in the banyan's shade—
dark in the daytime and dead still at night.

   * Kweilin: "Cinnamon Forest".

Entrance Fee

This jail collects an entrance fee.
The minimum is fifty yüan.
If you've got nothing to disburse,
trouble will dog your every step.

?!

Those forty days of utter waste.
Those forty days of pains untold.
Now they'll send me back to Liuchow.
Can any man endure it all?

?

'Liuchow, Kweilin, and now back to Liuchow.
They've kicked me back and forth—a soccer ball.
They've dragged a guiltless man all through Kwangsi.
Will these comings and goings ever end?

AT THE POLITICAL BUREAU OF THE FOURTH WAR ZONE

Hauled through all thirteen districts of Kwangsi
Time after time locked up in eighteen jails.
Tell me—what crime have I been guilty of?
Of staunch devotion to my people's cause.

MORNING SCENE

Each dawn the sun emerges from a peak.
It sets all hills aglow with a red fire.
But shadows still lie thick before the gate—
the sun is yet to reach inside the jail.

CH'ING-MING

Pure Brightness Day—it drizzles on and on.*
Jail inmates feel a wrench within their souls.
"But where is freedom to be found?" they ask.
The guard points to the yamen far away.

* Ch'ing-ming ("Pure Brightness") is the Chinese spring festival when people tend family graves and offer sacrifices to the dead.
This poem is patterned on a well-known quatrain by Tu Mu (803-852), a poet of the Late T'ang period: *Pure Brightness Day—it drizzles on and on./ The traveler feels a wrench within his soul./ "Where can one find a liquor shop?" he asks./ The herdboy points to a village far off.*

EVENING SCENE

A rose comes out in bloom, then fades away.
It lives and dies, uncared for by the world.
Its wafting fragrance seeps into the jail,
and to the prisoners it airs its grief.

RESTRICTIONS

To live unfree is the ultimate curse.
Even your bowel movements are controlled.
When the door is unlocked, no bellyache.
When your belly complains, the door is closed.

SLEEPLESS NIGHTS

All through those sleepless nights that would not end,
I wrote more than a hundred prison poems.
I wrote each quatrain, then put down the pen
to gaze at freedom's sky through prison bars.

ENDLESS RAIN

Nine days of rain, one day of sun.
Heaven above just doesn't care.
All tattered shoes, mud-splattered feet—
still I must walk and slog ahead.

Regrets for Lost Time

On purpose Heaven blocks a fighter's path.
Eight months I've wasted wearing cangue and cuffs.
Each day is worth a thousand pounds of gold.
When can I ever hope to be set free?

Autumn Feelings

I

The Dipper lies atop the hills—it's ten.
The cricket chirps and chirps, announcing fall.
In jail who cares if autumn comes or goes?
When one will get released is all that counts.

II

Last year in early autumn I walked free.
This year I find myself locked up in jail.
To help my people, what have I achieved?
I'd say this autumn's worthy of the last!

Allowed to Walk in the Prison Yard

They're soft as cotton, legs so long unused.
I lurch and stagger, trying hard to walk.
But soon enough I hear the warden shout:
"Hey you, come back! No more loafing around!"

Autumn Night

Soldiers stand guard with rifles at the gate.
Above, the moon drifts off on rags of clouds.
Bedbugs crawl here and there like army tanks.

Mosquitoes swarm and flee like fighter planes.
Beyond a thousand miles my heart goes home.
A tangled skein of sorrows weaves my dream.
Guiltless, I've languished a whole year in jail.
Pen dipped in tears, I write my prison poem.

On Reading the "Anthology of A Thousand Poets"

They used to sing of nature's charms—
hills, streams, mists, flowers, snow, moon, and wind.
Today, a poem must have steel.
A poet must learn to wage war.

Before A Landscape

Some branches draw a portrait of Chang Fei.
The sun glows red like Kuan Yü's stalwart heart.*
No news out of my country for a year.
Day after day I wait for word from home.

* Chang Fei and Kuan Yü were the two friends who helped Liu Pei triumph over his rivals and found the Shu Han dynasty in Szechuan, China, during the first centuries of the Christian era. All historical personages, they became fictionalized and idealized in *San Kuo Chih* (The Romance of the Three Kingdoms). Ho Chi Minh perhaps casts himself in the role of Liu Pei and thinks of his comrades back in Vietnam as Chang Fei and Kuan Yü.

The Weather Is Clearing Up

Things move in cycles—such is nature's law.
After the stormy days come days of calm.
The world has promptly changed its rain-soaked garb.
All hills and forests spread brocade to dry.
Warm sun and gentle breeze—flowers flash their smiles.

Tall trees and sparkling boughs—birds chat away.
Men join all myriad beings and rejoice.
The sweet follows the bitter, as a rule.

August 29, 1942
to
September 10, 1943

A Walk in the Mountains Upon Release from Prison

Clouds hug the mountains, mountains hug the clouds.
The river shines—a mirror clear of dust.
Restless, I walk alone on the West Range.
Gazing southward, I think of some old friends.

NOTES

PREFACE TO THE BOOK

1. For brief autobiographical essays by revolutionary leaders dealing with prison experiences, see Nguyen Duy Trinh et al., *In the Enemy's Net* (Hanoi, 1962). Several essays are also quite relevant in Ho Chi Minh et al., *A Heroic People* (Hanoi, 1965).

2. Dang Thai Mai, a prominent literary critic since the 1930s, mentions the writings of Cao Ba Nha, Doan Trung, Cao Ba Quat and Hoang Phan Thai. See his *Van Tho Cach Mang Viet Nam Dau The Ky XX* (*Vietnam's Revolutionary Prose and Poetry in the Early Twentieth Century*) (Hanoi, 1964), p. 117.

3. For translations of some of these works, see the following: " 'With the Only Weapons We Have' . . . Resistance in Saigon's Prisons," *Indochina Chronicle*, No. 40 (April 1975); *Eleven Poems of Political Prisoners* (Fullerton, Cal., Union of Vietnamese in the United States, 1974); Phuong Que, "We Must Keep Our Children," *Thoi Bao Ga*, No. 54 (December 1974); and Jacqui Chagnon and Don Luce (compilers), *Of Quiet Courage: Poems from Viet-Nam* (Washington, D.C., 1974).

INTRODUCTION TO *PRISON NOTES*

1. For a more detailed discussion of the life and times of Phan Boi Chau see David G. Marr, *Vietnamese Anticolonialism, 1885-1925* (University of California Press, 1971). Chapters 4-6 and 8-10 are especially relevant.

2. Phan Boi Chau wrote prolifically, so that *Nguc Trung Thu* can only be considered a schematic and hasty introduction to his writings. Other important works still extant of the pre-1914 period include: *Viet-Nam Vong Quoc Su* (*History of the Loss of Vietnam*); *Hai Ngoai Huyet Thu* (*Overseas Book Inscribed in Blood*); *Viet-Nam Quoc Su Khao* (*A Study of Vietnam's National History*); *Tan Viet-Nam* (*New Vietnam*); *Khuyen Quoc Dan Tu Tro Du Hoc Van* (*Encouragement to Citizens to Contribute for Overseas Study*); and *Tuong Trung Nu Vuong* (*A Play Concerning Queen Trung*).

3. Oiwa Makoto, *Annan Minzoku Undōshi Gaisetsu* (*A Historical Survey of Annamese Nationalist Movements*) (Tokyo[?], Guroria Sosaete, 1941).

4. Phan Boi Chau, *Nguc Trung Thu* (*Prison Notes*) trans., Dao Trinh Nhat, (Saigon, 1950). This is the basic text employed for translation to English here, with cross-checking of portions contained in available later anthologies.

5. Georges Boudarel, "Phan Boi Chau: Memoires." *France-Asie/Asia*, Vol. 22, No. 3/4, pp. 3-210. Two printings are available in *quoc-ngu*: Phan

Boi Chau Nien Bieu (*Year to Year Activities of Phan Boi Chau*) (Hanoi, 1957); and *Tu Phan* (*Self-judgment*), (Hue, 1956).

6. Vu Dinh Lien, *et al.*, eds., *Hop Tuyen Tho Van Viet-Nam 1885-1930* (*A Collection of Vietnamese Poetry and Prose, 1885-1930*). (Hanoi: 1963), p. 443.

7. Marr, pp. 279-290.

PRISON NOTES

1. Albert Sarraut.

2. A common expression among nationalists of the time, although the figure was probably closer to 20 million.

3. By Western solar calendar reckoning Phan was born *five* years after the French occupation of three provinces in the southern region of Vietnam.

4. An apparent reference to *Ong Troi*, the omnipresent Being (or Force) in traditional Sino-Vietnamese thought who often seemed to determine man's destiny.

5. A reference to the European Enlightenment.

6. Nineteenth century Vietnam generally patterned its examination system after that of the Chinese, which in turn had first been developed during the T'ang dynasty (618-906 A.D.). See Alexander Woodside, *Vietnam and the Chinese Model* (Cambridge, Mass., 1971), for a discussion of the examination system under the Nguyen dynasty.

7. Can Vuong, literally "loyalty to the king," is the name given to the monarchist armed guerrilla movement against the French led by a minority of mandarins and scholars during the decade following the flight of King Ham Nghi in 1885.

8. The northern region of Vietnam, called Tonkin by the French.

9. Truong Cong Dinh, also known as Truong Dinh, born in 1820 in central Vietnam, became a wealthy southern landowner and military commander. When Phan Thanh Gian ceded the Mekong Delta area to the French in 1862, Truong Cong Dinh led an anti-French resistance until he was killed by one of his former followers in 1864.

10. The southern region of Vietnam, called Cochinchina by the French.

11. General Nguyen Tri Phuong led King Tu Duc's army against the French at Danang with some success in 1858. But in 1861 he was forced by the French to retreat from his fortifications at Chi Hoa, near Saigon. In 1873 he was gravely wounded as the French seized Hanoi. Captured, he refused all offers of medicine and food from the French in order to commit suicide.

12. Nguyen Xuan On, also called Nguyen On, was born in 1825. He achieved the rank of *Tien Si* (doctorate) after passing the metropolitan exams in 1871. In 1885 he led the Can Vuong uprisings in Nghe An but was captured by the French two years later and finally died in jail in 1889.

13. This may be a reference to Dinh Cong Trang, who led a staunch effort at position defense at Ba Dinh in Thanh Hoa province, December 1886-January 1887.

14. Generally known as Phu Dong Thien Vuong, or the "Celestial Prince of Phu Dong village." This is an important Vietnamese epic folktale, dating back perhaps to the pre-Chinese colonial period, in which a three-year-old peasant boy grows to giant size upon hearing the king's buglers calling for assistance to repel foreign invaders from the state of An. Mounted upon a huge, fire-breathing iron horse and swinging mighty sticks of bamboo, the boy drives out the foreigners. He then returns fondly to his native village for one last look, before ascending to heaven on his iron horse.

15. No information is presently available on either of these individuals.

16. Phan Dinh Phung, who in 1877 became a scholar of the highest rank, joined the Can Vuong movement in 1885 and led a guerrilla resistance against the French in his native Ha Tinh province. In 1894 he died from dysentery as the French closed in on his last remaining outpost.

17. Presumably Bastille Day, July 14, when the French colonials were likely to have their guard down, conducting parades, giving banquets and otherwise carousing.

18. An area in the Nghe An/Ha Tinh region of central Vietnam.

19. Important landmarks in Nghe An province.

20. Nghe-Tinh is the common abbreviation when speaking of the two provinces.

21. No information is available to further identify these personalities.

22. Often known under the pseudonym Ngu Hai, Dang Thai Than was also a native of Nghe An. He met his death in 1910 when French and collaborationist Vietnamese militia surrounded his home. In a letter from Pham Mai Lam that Phan quotes in the *Nien Bieu* (*Phan Boi Chau Nien Bieu/ Year to Year Activities of Phan Boi Chau*) (Hanoi: Van Su Dia, 1957), hereinafter referred to as NB, p. 129, or see Georges Boudarel, "Phan Bol Chau: Memoires." *France-Asie-Asia* Vol. 22, No. 3/4, hereinafter referred to as Boudarel, p. 123, it is reported that after burning his papers, Dang fired at a French soldier, then turned his gun on a Vietnamese soldier. "I could kill you too," he said, "but I don't want to kill men of my own race," whereupon he pressed his pistol to his throat and killed himself.

23. In the *Nien Bieu*, Phan adds that Dang Van Ba was a native of Ha Tinh province.

24. Nguyen Thanh joined the Can Vuong resistance when he was on his way to take the regional exams in 1885 and then afterwards joined Phan Boi Chau in the Duy Tan Hoi. He died a prisoner on Con Son island in late 1911 or early 1912.

25. Nguyen Than was less sympathetic to other Can Vuong leaders. A collaborator mandarin, he is better remembered for digging up Phan Dinh Phung's fresh grave, burning the corpse, and firing the ashes out of a cannon in the traditional manner reserved for common thieves.

26. Le Vo was also known as Dat Truc.

27. In fact, he had been exiled by the French to Réunion Island in the Indian Ocean.

28. Literally "Royal Highness," referring here to Gia Long, the founder of the Nguyen dynasty. Gia Long's descendant here is Prince Cuong De.

29. In a later biographical interview, Prince Cuong De mentioned that this meeting took place at the home of Tran Xuan Han, son of Tran Xuan Soan who had followed Ton That Thuyet into exile in China after the failure of the Can Vuong movement.

30. Phan writes in the *Nien Bieu* that he visited Hoang Hoa Tham in Phon Xuong in the fall of 1902.

31. Better known as De Tham, Hoang Hoa Tham was a peasant who grew up during violent times in the mountains of Yen The, not far from the Chinese border. His vigilante activities took on a political character as he harassed the French and then supported the resistance of Phan Boi Chau and other post-Can Vuong anticolonial leaders. He was finally killed by the French in 1913.

32. This man is probably Nguyen Quang Bich, also known as Ngo Quang Bich. A member of the highest rank of the scholar-gentry (*Tien Si*), Bich worked together with Liu Yung-fu's Black Flags in resistance against the French. He was an active leader of the Can Vuong resistance. Although Phan here says he was killed in battle, he is elsewhere reported to have died of natural causes. *Hop Tuyen Tho Van Viet-Nam (1858-1930)*, Vu Dinh Lien et al., eds., (Hanoi, 1963).

33. A leader of the Can Vuong movement, Nguyen Thien Thuat originally went to China in 1888 to seek assistance from Liu Yung-fu and the Black Flags.

34. No other information is available on Nguyen Cu.

35. Nguyen Dien later was to betray Phan and become an agent for the French *Sûreté*. Boudarel writes that he was killed by Tran Huu Luc and Dang Tu Kinh who stabbed him with a chopping knife that they had borrowed from a sympathetic Chinese woman (NB pp. 132-133, Boudarel, pp. 125-126). Below (p. 35) Phan reports that around 1908 the French stepped up their recruitment of agents to spy on the activities of Vietnamese students in Japan.

36. In Chau Doc province near the Cambodian border.

37. Nguyen Huan, whose full name is Nguyen Huu Huan, was a scholar who led an armed resistance against French efforts in the mid-nineteenth century to annex areas of the Mekong Delta, particularly Tan An and My Tho.

38. In the *Nien Bieu* (NB p. 39, Boudarel, p. 34), Phan adds more importance to this trip south adding that he met Tran Nhut Tri at the That Son (Seven Mountain) Pagoda. Tri was to raise funds for Phan from wealthy southern landowners. Phan also met Nguyen Than Hien in Sadec, who, he reports, was to work with him "for more than seven years." Phan may have been less specific about his trip to the south in *Nguc Trung Thu* in an effort to conceal the identity of his supporters there.

39. When the French installed Dong Khanh on the throne in 1886 they made a convention with him whereby they stationed French administrators or *Résidents* in each province of Annam.

40. Phan passed the regional exams in 1900 with highest honors but failed the metropolitan exams in Hue in 1904. His literary reputation, however, far surpassed any that might have derived from scholarly rank.

41. In Vietnamese, Dong Cac. Boudarel translates it as "Grand Chancellor."

42. This may be a literary allusion, or simply a metaphor to reinforce his point that nobody could have swayed these court officials.

43. Phan Chau Trinh, also known as Phan Chu Trinh or Phan Tay Ho, observed the Can Vuong movement as a boy. Later, in 1901, he went on to pass the metropolitan exams. His strategy for Vietnam's future differed somewhat from that of Phan Boi Chau who wrote in the *Nien Bieu* (*NB* p. 86, Boudarel, p. 81): "Phan Chu Trinh spoke out strongly in favor of democratic rights and overthrowing the monarchy with no mention of throwing out the French. His strategy was to rely on France to blaze the trail of progress [for Vietnam]."

44. Tran Quy Cap was a follower of Phan Chau Trinh. Cap was accused of treason and chopped in half at the waist in Nha Trang in 1908.

45. These are all former Vietnamese dynasties. The Dinh and the Le dynasties are particularly remembered for expelling Chinese invaders.

46. The Ch'in ruled China from 221-207 B.C. and the Sui from 581-618 A.D.

47. Phan is particularly close to indiscretion in this passage, since at the time of his imprisonment in January 1914 much thought was being given by his comrades to cultivating Vietnamese enlisted men in French colonial units. During World War I there were indeed several significant uprisings. Assuming the French *Sûreté* was able to acquire a copy of *Nguc Trung Thu*, this passage must have been especially interesting to them.

48. Apparently a Chinese classical reference.

49. Phan is apparently in error here, as the historical record shows that the Chinese won quite a victory at Lang Son, although they did indeed lose the war and were forced to sign a humiliating treaty with France.

50. Sometime in 1904 the Association took the name *Duy Tan Hoi* (Reformation Society). Yet nowhere in the text does Phan refer to the group formally, always preferring to use *hoi* (association) or *dang* (party). By 1912 the Association took the name *Viet-Nam Quang Phuc Hoi* (Vietnam Restoration Society).

51. Liu Yung-fu (in Vietnamese Luu Vinh Phuc) first came to Vietnam in 1865 after the defeat of the Taiping rebellion. As his band grew they became known as the Black Flags. When the French threatened his activities in the northern reaches of the Red River Delta, Liu fought back, often in combination with Vietnamese groups, and together they succeeded in killing Francis Garnier in 1873 and Captain Rivière and 32 other Frenchmen in 1883. Twenty years later, "retired" in south China, Liu offered his moral support and the wisdom of his experience to Phan Boi Chau and his followers.

52. It was at Cau Giay that Liu led the forces that killed Captain Rivière in 1883, a serious psychological setback for the French.

53. Liang Ch'i-ch'ao, a leader of the Chinese reform movement, escaped in 1898 to Japan where he was a leader of the Chinese students then studying in Japan.

54. Inukai Tsuyoshi was a Japanese party politician, closely associated with Okuma Shigenobu, who led a complex bureaucratic, capitalist and intellectual opposition to the ruling oligarchy in the period. He was assassinated in 1932.

55. See "Hai van kien ngoai giao dau tien cua Phan Boi Chau" (The

first two foreign letters of Phan Boi Chau). Translation and comments: Chuong Thau. *Nghien Cuu Lich Su*, No. 90 pp. 61-64, (Sept. 1966).

56. Not sharing the same spoken language, Phan and Liang communicated by writing in Chinese characters, the language of study for both of them.

57. In the *Nien Bieu*, however, (NB p. 54, Boudarel, p. 49) Phan writes that at this first meeting Liang gave him some solid advice for obtaining independence for Vietnam:

1) build up the strength of the country, which Liang defined as the zeal (*dan khi*), intellect (*dan tri*), and talent (*nhan tai*) of the people;

2) seek military aid and the help of troops from Kwangtung and Kwangsi;

3) seek diplomatic recognition from Japan.

Fulfilling the latter two conditions would be useless, Liang warned, without having fulfilled the first. It is more likely that Liang gave this advice during Phan's second trip to Japan, as he has written later on in this account (pp. 35-6).

58. According to the *Nien Bieu* (NB p. 58, Boudarel, p. 52), Phan wrote *Viet-Nam Vong Quoc Su* after a second meeting with Liang, during which Liang emphasized to Phan that he should write many militant articles alerting the world to the French attempts "to kill your country and your people."

59. In Vietnamese *Tan Bo*, actually at that time called the *Kenseihonto* or Orthodox Constitutional Party.

60. In Vietnamese, *Hoi Dong A Dong Van*.

61. The *Nien Bieu* cites this man as Ly Tue, who was to serve from this point on as an important liaison agent for Phan and the *Duy Tan Hoi*. Here in the *Nguc Trung Thu* Phan writes that he did not meet Ly Tue until later (p. 34).

62. Boudarel, in his translation of the *Nien Bieu*, refers to the province chief as Doan, although there is no such reference in the original *Nien Bieu*.

63. Tran Dong Phong, according to the *Nien Bieu* (NB p. 124, Boudarel, p. 115), was the son of a wealthy southern landlord. He joined Phan to study in Japan but committed suicide in 1908, shamed by his rich father's refusal to support financially the anticolonial struggle.

64. Boudarel notes that such an amount would weigh 5.5 kilos, or about 12 pounds. (Boudarel, p. 42).

65. Nguyen Thuc Canh, also known as Tran Huu Long and Tran Trong Khac, was the eldest son of one of Phan's teachers, Nguyen Thuc Tu. Long active with Phan, Nguyen Thuc Canh eventually went to study in Germany, where Phan sent him money from time to time.

66. Ly Tue had been in Son La prison for two years when Phan wrote this. He was released about 1921. He and Phan met again in 1938, the year Ly Tue died.

67. Luong Lap Nham, also known as Luong Ngoc Quyen, was the son of Luong Van Can, a wealthy Hanoi silk merchant and one of the leaders in 1907 in establishing the *Dong Kinh Nghia Thuc* (the Nontuition School of the Eastern Capital). Luong Lap Nham helped instigate the Thai Nguyen uprising of 1917 and was killed in the early fighting.

68. The terms used her, *dantri* and *nhantai*, have a rich history in both Chinese and Sino-Vietnamese writings. One grapples with the question of popular political consciousness while the other deals with general education and specialized technical training.

69. Phan, below, calls this treatise *Khuyen Thanh Nien Du Hoc* (*Advice to Youth to Study Abroad*). In the *Nien Bieu*, however, the treatise is called *Khuyen Quoc Dan Tu Tro Du Hoc Van* (*Encouragement to Citizens to Contribute for Overseas Study*) and in the *Tu Phan* version it is called *Khuyen Quoc Dan Du Hoc Van* (*Advice to the People to Study Abroad*). There is a Vietnamese translation of the treatise, which was originally written in *chu nom*, in *Van Tho Cach Mang Viet Nam Dan The Ky XX* by Dang Thai Mai (Hanoi, 1964).

70. A Chinese classical reference.

71. Luong Nghi Khanh was the brother of Luong Lap Nham (fn. 67).

72. These appear to be pseudonyms. No other information is available on them.

73. Champa was a maritime kingdom with highly developed forms of Hindu and Buddhist civilization that flourished along the coast of central and southern Vietnam from the second century A.D. until virtually exterminated by Vietnamese southern expansion in the fifteenth century.

74. Chenla, a predominantly Hindu civilization that appeared in the middle of the sixth century in what is now northern Cambodia and southern Laos, yielded in the eighth century to the Kingdom of Angkor.

75. In 39 A.D. the Trung sisters, Trung Trac and Trung Nhi, led a rebellion against the Chinese overlords who controlled Vietnam at that time. Although the sisters maintained Vietnamese independence for only two years, they henceforth became important symbols of the Vietnamese struggle for national liberation.

76. The Le dynasty (1418-1802) was for its first 90 years one of Vietnam's most glorious periods. Le Loi, who founded the dynasty in 1418 and drove out the Ming Chinese invaders ten years later, has become one of Vietnam's most revered national heroes.

77. No further information available.

78. Later on, in Hangchow in 1918, Phan Ba Ngoc persuaded Phan Boi Chau to write an essay mildly conciliatory to Albert Sarraut's idea of Franco-Vietnamese collaboration. Phan Ba Ngoc returned to Vietnam and showed the essay to the French. The French, impressed with the essay, offered Phan Boi Chau a high but token position at the Hue court if he were to promise to renounce his revolutionary ways. Phan refused. Nevertheless, Cuong De was so enraged by Phan Ba Ngoc's act that in 1922 he had him assassinated in Hangchow.

79. Probably a pseudonym.

80. Ngo Duc Ke, also known as Tap Xuyen, passed the metropolitan exams in 1901. He was an avid reader of the Chinese reformists Liang Ch'i-ch'ao and K'ang Yu-wei. He was sent to Con Son prison island in 1908. After his release in 1921 he edited a small *quoc ngu* periodical in Hanoi.

81. In the *Nien Bieu* (NB pp. 83-84, Boudarel, p. 77) this meeting in Hanoi is said to have taken place after the meeting in Bac Ninh.

82. No other information available.

83. No other information available on these personalities.

84. Boudarel, in his translation of *Nien Bieu* (NB p. 70, n. 81), explains that the Vietnam Merchant Association was located in "an inn situated in

Kowloon (Hong Kong) which put up those newly arrived from Vietnam. Vo Man Kien met them at the boat, took them to a barber where he had them cut their hair, bought them European clothes, saw to the changing of their money and the purchase of their tickets for Japan."

85. In the *Nien Bieu* Phan adds that "at that time in Hong Kong we had established a small group and four or five of our number had learned English. But there were very few of us, about 40 altogether, all working for the French pirates. Three or four worked as secretaries and interpreters, all the rest boys or cooks" (NB pp. 76-77, Boudarel, pp. 70-71).

86. In the *Nien Bieu* Phan explains that the *Tan Viet-Nam Cong Hien* (or *Viet-Nam Cong Hien Hoi* as he calls it there) was a student organization designed to give order and discipline to student life outside school. The Association took on the forms of a government with a president (Cuong De) and four ministries responsible for finances, discipline, foreign relations and administration.

87. In this Treaty, signed in 1907, Japan and France agreed to recognize and respect each other's colonial possessions in Asia.

88. Ho Hoc Lam, also known as Ho Hinh Son, according to the *Nien Bieu* (NB p. 147, Boudarel, p. 139) entered an officers' school in Peking in 1912. By 1917 he was in Hangchow and often the host of Phan.

89. Nguyen Tieu Dau, also known as Nguyen Ba Trac, went to infantry school in Kwangsi, according to the *Nien Bieu* (NB p. 111 Boudarel, p. 103).

90. Dang Quoc Kieu had come to Japan to study in the winter of 1907-1908, according to the *Nien Bieu* (NB p. 78, Boudarel, p. 72).

91. See note 65.

92. Hoang Dinh Tuan, also known as Nguyen Ke Chi, actually became a naturalized Chinese citizen in order to stay in Japan, according to Phan in the *Nien Bieu* (NB pp. 104-105, Boudarel, p. 98). Posing as a Cantonese he attended a Japanese school with a Japanese government scholarship. Later he taught in Peking, always helping Phan in his diplomatic activities there.

93. Each of these is a specific reference to a story in the Chinese classics.

94. In the *Nien Bieu* (NB p. 126, Boudarel p. 120) Phan writes that the sum of money was 2,500 piasters, 2,100 of which he entrusted to Dang Tu Kinh and Dang Ngo Sinh to buy weapons in Tokyo. According to Phan they bought 100 Meiji-30 rifles for cash, at 20 piasters apiece, and 400 more on credit. These were the rifles Japan had used to defeat Russia in 1905, but by 1909 they had been replaced by a new model.

95. *i.e.*, the Tung-meng-hui.

96. Apparently the Vietnamese transliteration of the name of a Chinese contact.

97. Phan writes in the *Nien Bieu* (NB p. 127, Boudarel, p. 121) that his trip to Singapore preceded his trip to Siam and that the shipping price quoted to him was 1,000 piasters—a price "impossible" to pay but one that he "reluctantly" accepted.

98. On the other hand, the *Nien Bieu* (NB p. 130, Boudarel p. 123) has it that once it was obvious the weapons were not going to be useful inside Vietnam, Phan donated the bulk to the Chinese Tung-meng-hui.

99. No further information available.

100. No further information available.

101. Reference to an ancient Vietnamese folktale in which Phieu Mau (god-mother) is fondly recalled as a provider of rice.

102. Ngo Sanh, also known under such pseudonyms as Dang Ngo Sinh, Dang Nguyen Can, Thai Son, Dang Thai Son and Dang Thuc Hoa, is mentioned by Phan in the *Nien Bieu* (NB p. 48, Boudarel, p. 43) as the mandarin in charge of education (*doc hoc*) in Nghe An in 1905. A longtime follower of Phan, he suggested in 1906 the formation of associations of peasants, merchants and students as a way of making the Association more widely known.

103. A Chinese historical figure.

104. See Boudarel (Boudarel, p. 129, n. 135) for a discussion of the location of this town.

105. *Quoc ngu* is the Vietnamese language written in romanized script. It was developed in the seventeenth century by European Jesuit missionaries in order to make literacy and therefore the scriptures more available to Catholic converts. By the early 1900's, *quoc ngu* had been adopted by anticolonial leaders. They too realized it would allow the level of popular education (and therefore anticolonial consciousness) to rise progressively.

106. Le Thai To is the dynastic name for King Le Loi, founder of the Le dynasty (see note 76).

107. The Trung sisters (see note 75).

108. The army revolt in central China that sparked the 1911 Revolution.

109. Vietnamese transliterations of Chinese names.

110. Phan lists Truong Ke's full name in the *Nien Bieu* as Truong Ke Canh (NB p. 119).

111. Vietnamese transliteration of Chinese name.

112. This treatise was written in praise of those who, in 1908, attempted a military coup in Hanoi through a few key military moves and the poisoning of several hundred French soldiers. The plot failed, however, and most participants were captured. Thirteen of them were executed.

113. Do Chon Thiet, also known as Do Chan Thiet and referred to by Phan in the *Nien Bieu* (NB p. 161) as Do Co Quang and in the *Tu Phan* (pp. 165-66) as Dan Co Quang, was a poet active in the *Dong Kinh Nghia Thuc*, a school set up by Vietnamese reformists in 1907.

114. Gia Cat Khong Minh was known as a great strategist in the ancient Chinese legend of the *Three Kingdoms*.

115. Also known as Mai Son or Dinh Than, Nguyen Thuong Hien, a successful candidate in the metropolitan exams, joined Phan in Japan in 1907. Hien took over leadership of the *Viet-Nam Quang Phuc Hoi*, such as it was, while in jail from 1914 to 1917.

116. The government in Peking at the time was that of Yuan Shih-k'ai.

117. Mai Lao Bang, also known as Gia Chau, led the first group of Catholic Vietnamese students to Japan in 1908. In 1912 he was a member of the executive committee of the *Viet-Nam Quang Phuc Hoi*.

118. *Nom*, or *chu nom*, was a cumbersome Vietnamese modification of

Chinese characters (plus many original characters) that allowed the reader to associate the sound and syntax of the Vietnamese language with the written script. As might be expected, *nom* was particularly useful for writing Vietnamese poetry, or for recording popular stories and epigrams, whereas classical Chinese remained in use for most other purposes—until both were supplanted by *quoc ngu* in the early twentieth century.

119. Hung Vuong is the name given to the legendary first dynasty of Vietnamese rulers.

120. i.e., Le Loi.

INTRODUCTION TO *PRISON DIARY*

1. Nguyen was Ho Chi Minh's real surname. Until about ten years of age his name was Nguyen Sinh Cung, later changed by his family to Nguyen Tat Thanh. After departing from Vietnam at about 21 he adopted a bewildering variety of pseudonyms. Until World War II, however, he was best known as Nguyen Ai Quoc. Upon setting off for Chungking in August 1942, he identified himself as Ho Chi Minh, and this is the name he retained until his death in 1969.

2. For further discussion of this incident see David G. Marr, *Vietnamese Anticolonialism* (Berkeley, 1971), pp. 260-61.

3. Tran Dan Tien, *Doi Hoat Dong Cua Ho Chu Tich* (Chairman Ho's Active Life), n.p., n.d., pp. 72-73.

4. For this English version of Ho Chi Minh's collection of prison poems, Huynh Sanh Thong is a specialist in Vietnamese literature whose blank verse which includes the original Chinese language text as well as literal and literary renditions into Vietnamese. He also consulted earlier English versions by Aileen Palmer (*The Prison Diary of Ho Chi Minh*, New York: Bantam, 1971). Huynh Sanh Thong is a specialist in Vietnamese literature whose blank verse translation of Nguyen Du, *The Tale of Kieu* was published by Random House and by Vintage Books in 1973.

5. For further discussion, brief yet still quite interesting, see the exchange between Reed Whittemore and Huynh Sanh Thong in the January 1972 issue of *Intellectual Digest*, entitled "Was Ho Chi Minh a bad poet?" A more detailed exposition is contained in Hoai Thanh, 'Doc Nhat Ky Trong Tu,' *Nghien Cuu Van Hoc* (Hanoi) No. 4 (1961), pp. 1-11.

6. It is fascinating here to compare and contrast Ho Chi Minh's quatrain with the following poem by the famous fifteenth century Vietnamese leader, writer and moralist, Nguyen Trai:

Inside the gourd, a round shape water takes.
For good or ill, all fit into some mold.
Live near the rich—you'll feed on bran galore.
Fall in with thieves—you'll rue it and eat stick.
Befriend a fool—you'll swell the ranks of fools.
Meet clever men—you'll learn their clever tricks.
Mix with low folk—you'll act just like low folk.

Get black with ink, get red with cinnabar.

(Translation by Huynh Sanh Thong, from poems by Nguyen Trai being prepared for publication.)

INDEX

Can Vuong movement, 12, 13, 14, 15, 18, 28
Canton, 28, 40, 48-49, 51, 53, 61
Champa, 39
Chang Fa-kwei, 64
Ch'en Chiung-minh, 51, 53
Chenla, 39
China: Vietnamese relations with, 10, 24, 59, 70, 77, 87; border with Vietnam, 27, 40-41, 52, 62; 1911 Revolution, 3-4, 75; Tung-meng-hui, 47, 50; Kuomintang, 4, 63-64, 77; Chinese Communist Party, 63; Phan Boi Chau in, 4, 6, 9, 27-29, 40, 43, 47-49, 50-56; Ho Chi Minh in, 60-64, 70ff; anti-Japanese struggle, 86
Chinese written language, 29, 30, 86
Comintern, ix
Con Son prison, x, 7, 59, 105
Cuong De, 17-19, 24, 32-34, 38, 45, 105
Dang Ngo Sanh. *See* Ngo Sanh
Dang Nguyen Can. *See* Ngo Sanh
Dang Quoc Kieu, 46
Dang Thai Than, 15, 16, 34, 42, 43, 47-48
Dang Tu Kinh, 26, 32, 34, 38, 49, 51, 102, 106
Dang Tu Man, 43, 47
Dang Van Ba, 15, 16
Dao Tien, 20
Dat Truc. *See* Le Vo
De Tham. *See* Hoang Hoa Tham
Dinh Cong Trang, 100
Dinh Van Chat, 12
Dinh Xuan Sang, 12
Do Chan Thiet, 52
Dong Du movement, 36-39, 43-45, 59
Dong Thien Vuong. *See* Phu Dong Thien Vuong
Duy Tan Hoi: formation, 18-19, 25; objectives, 31-32; activities, 42-44, 47; destruction, 47-48
Education: traditional examination system, 10-11, 14, 25, 29, 59; Western/modern learning, 10, 25, 29, 32-33, 39, 59; French control of colonial, 36; overseas, 36, 43-45
French colonial administration, 19-20, 36, 60

French security system, 3, 5, 9, 22, 26-27, 33-34, 37, 40, 43, 44-46, 47-48, 53, 61, 62, 103
Fukushima Yasumasa, 31-32, 38
Ha Thanh Liet Si (*Martyrs of Hanoi*), 52
Ha Van My, 13
Hai Ngoai Huyet Thu (*Overseas Book Written in Blood*), by Phan Boi Chau, 38-39
Haiphong, 26, 33, 34
Ham Nghi, King, 11, 12, 17
Hangchow, 105, 106
Hanoi, 41, 42, 61, 112
Ho Chi Minh: historical accomplishments, ix, 66; as youth, 59-60; travel overseas, 60-63; imprisoned in Kwangsi, 63-64, 69ff; *Nguc Trung Nhat Ky* characterized, 64-66; *Nguc Trung Nhat Ky* translated, 69-98; political philosophy of, 64-66, 85, 86, 97; philosophy of life, 69, 75, 76, 77, 85, 86, 89, 90, 91, 92, 97-98; appreciation of nature, 73, 74, 77, 79, 83, 87, 94, 95, 97; appreciation of music, 71, 72, 84; appreciation of food, 72, 76, 78, 88, 89; on sleep, 71, 79, 80, 84, 95; on labor, 88; on fetters, 72, 80, 81, 82, 87, 96; on illness, 85, 92-93
Ho Hoc Lam, 45
Hoang Dinh Tuan, 46
Hoang Hoa Tham, 18-19, 40, 42, 47
Hoang Trong Mau, 52, 53
Hong Kong, 27-28, 29, 38, 43, 47, 48, 50, 62
Hu Han-min, 51, 53
Hue, 11, 19, 26, 34, 59-60
Hung Vuong, 55
Huynh Thuc Khang, 7
Indochinese Communist Party, 62-63, 65
Inukai Tsuyoshi, 31, 37-38
Japan: Russo-Japanese War, 22-23, 32; Phan Boi Chau seeks support from, 24, 30-32; first Phan Boi Chau trip to, 29-32; Vietnamese study in, 36-39, 43-45, 59; treaty with France, 45; Ho Chi Minh attitude towards, 86
Kashiwabara Buntaro, 31-32
Khuyen Thanh Nien Du Hoc (*Advice to*

Youth to Study Abroad), by Phan Boi Chau, 37
Kuomintang, 4, 63-64, 77
Le dynasty, 39
Le Loi, 49, 55
Le Vo, 16, 43, 48
Liang Ch'i-ch'ao, 5, 30-31, 35-36
Liang San-ch'i, 41-42
Lien A Xo Ngon (Modest Proposal for an Asian Alliance), by Phan Boi Chau, 50
Literature: Vietnamese texts in Chinese, 4, 86-87, 94; nom, 54, 64, 105; quoc-ngu, 49-50, 64; T'ang poetic medium, 64; prison literature, ix-x; Phan Boi Chau as literary figure, 20, 46; literary quality of Nguc Trung Thu, 7; literary merits of Nguc Trung Nhat Ky, 65-66, 97, 108
Liu Yung-fu, 26, 28, 102
London, 60
Lung Chi-kuang, 4, 6, 9, 53-54
Luong Lap Nham, 35, 38
Luong Nghi Khanh, 38
Luong Ngoc Quyen. See Luong Lap Nham
Luong Van Can, 104
Luu Cau · Huyet Le Tan Thu (Ryukyu's Bitter Tears), by Phan Boi Chau, 20-21, 39
Ly Tue, 34-35, 104
Mai Lao Bang, 53-55
Mai Son. See Nguyen Thuong Hien
Monarchism, 17, 31-32, 103
Nghe An/Ha Tinh provinces, 13, 14, 33, 34, 39, 59, 62
Ngo Duc Ke, 42, 59
Ngo Sanh, 49, 106, 107
Ngu Hai. See Dang Thai Than
Nguc Trung Nhat Ky (Prison Diary), by Ho Chi Minh: characterized, 64-66; translated to English, 69-98
Nguc Trung Thu (Prison Notes), by Phan Boi Chau: 1914 composition of, 4; significance of, 4-7; comparison with Nien Bieu, 6; translated to English, 9-56
Nguyen Ai Quoc. See Ho Chi Minh
Nguyen Ba Trac, 46
Nguyen Bich, 18
Nguyen Cu, 18
Nguyen Dien, 18, 38
Nguyen Hai Than, 37, 51, 52
Nguyen Ham. See Nguyen Thanh
Nguyen Huan, 19
Nguyen Huu Huan. See Nguyen Huan
Nguyen Quang Bich. See Nguyen Bich
Nguyen Sinh Sac, 59, 60
Nguyen Than, 16
Nguyen Than Hien, 102
Nguyen Thang, 20
Nguyen Thanh, 16-17, 18
Nguyen Thien Thuat, 18, 28
Nguyen Thuat, 20
Nguyen Thuc Canh, 34, 38
Nguyen Thuong Hien, 53
Nguyen Tieu Dau. See Nguyen Ba Trac
Nguyen Trai, 108-109
Nguyen Tri Phuong, 12
Nguyen Xuan On, 12
Nhat Ky Trong Tu. See Nguc Trung Nhat Ky
Okuma Shigenobu, 31
Paris, 60
Peking, 45, 53
Phan Ba Ngoc, 40, 50, 53
Phan Boi Chau: historical accomplishments, ix, 3-4; as youth, 10-13; Can Vuong connections, 13-14; first trip overseas, 26-32; second trip overseas, 34-40; third trip overseas, 43-56; writes Nguc Trung Thu, 4-7; writes Nien Bieu, 6; Ho Chi Minh contact with, 59, 61-62; attitudes towards death, 9, 46, 54, 56
Phan Chu Trinh, 21, 38-39, 59, 60
Phan Dinh Phung, 13, 14, 40
Phu Dong Thien Vuong, 12
Political concepts: of Phan Boi Chau, 23-24, 36; of Liang Ch'i-ch'ao, 36, 104; of Ho Chi Minh, 64-66, 85, 86, 97; monarchism, 17, 31-32; loyalty, 17; "the People", 14, 16, 38; freedom/captivity, 55, 65, 69, 71, 74, 81, 84, 87, 90, 94, 96; perfectability of man, 65-66, 91
Political strategies: collaboration, 5; of Nguyen Thanh, 16-17; Liang Ch'i-ch'ao advice to Phan Boi Chau, 30-31, 35-36, 104; obtaining Japanese help, 31-32; of Duy Tan Hoi, 18-19, 25, 31-32, 42; of Phan Chu Trinh, 38; obtaining and using weapons, 12, 22, 24, 30, 34, 35, 36, 39, 40, 47, 48; obtaining and using money, 37, 47, 51, 52-53; Phan Boi Chau strategic assessment, 55-56
Prisons: political significance of, ix-x; literature in, ix-x; living conditions in, 71ff; on Con Son island, x, 7; in Canton, 4, 53-56; in Kwangsi, 63-64, 69ff
Quang Nam province, 15-16, 18, 24, 34
Quang Ngai province, 15-16, 34
Russo-Japanese War, 22-23, 32
Saigon, 10, 19, 60

Index

Shanghai, 29, 51, 61
Singapore, 47
Tan Viet-Nam Cong Hien (Vietnam Constitutionalist Association), 44
Tan Viet-Nam Ky Niem Luc (*Anniversary of the New Vietnam*), by Phan Boi Chau, 39
Tang Bat Ho, 24, 26-27, 37
Thai Son. *See* Ngo Sanh
Thailand, 47, 49-50, 52
Thanh Thai, King, 17
Toa Dobun Kai (East Asia Common Culture Society), 31
Toa Domei Kai (East Asia United League), 50
Tokyo, 31, 32, 35
Tran Dong Phong, 34
Tran Huu Luc, 102
Tran Nhut Tri, 102
Tran Quy Cap, 21
Tran The Hoa, 41
Tran Trong Khac, 46
Tran Van Luong, 12
Tran Xuan Soan, 102
Trung sisters, 39, 49-50

Truong Cong Dinh, 12, 19
Ts'en Ch'un-hsuan, 28-29
Tung-meng-hui, 47, 51, 53-98
Viet Minh, 62-4, 65, 84
Vietnam: south, 10, 19, 60; border with China, 27, 40-41, 52-62; relations with China, 10, 24, 59, 70, 77, 87. *See also* education; literature; monarchism; political concepts; political strategies; youth
Viet-Nam Cong Hien Hoi. *See* Tan Viet-Nam Cong Hien
Viet-Nam Vong Quoc Su (*History of the Loss of Vietnam*), by Phan Boi Chau, 30
Viet-Nam Quang Phuc Hoi (Society for the Restoration of Vietnam), 52-53
Viet-Nam Quoc Su Khao (*A Study of Vietnam's National History*), by Phan Boi Chau, 39
Viet-Nam Thuong Doan Cong Hoi (Vietnam Merchant Association), 43
Vuong Thuc Quy, 13
Yokohama, 29-31, 32, 35, 38
Youth, Vietnamese: Phan Boi Chau counsels, 29; travel to Japan, 35-9, 43-5